M000011536

60-SECOND ASSESSMENTS
TO IMPROVE YOUR PLANNING TODAY

ROLEK
RETIREMENT
PLANNING

—— THE ESSENTIALS EDITION ——

KYLE ROLEK

WITH RODNEY A. BROOKS

Rolek Retirement Planning
PHILADELPHIA, PENNSYLVANIA

Copyright © 2018 by Kyle Rolek.

All rights reserved. No part of this publication may be reproduced, distributed or transmitted in any form or by any means, including photocopying, recording, or other electronic or mechanical methods, without the prior written permission of the publisher, except in the case of brief quotations embodied in critical reviews and certain other noncommercial uses permitted by copyright law. For permission requests, write to the publisher.

Kyle Rolek/Rolek Retirement Planning
30 South 15th Street, 15th Floor
Philadelphia, PA 19102
www.rolekretirement.com

Rolek Retirement Planning / Kyle Rolek. —1st ed.
ISBN 978-1-7325570-0-0

Rolek Retirement Planning is an independent financial services firm that helps individuals with comprehensive retirement planning. Investment advisory services offered only by duly registered individuals through Rolek Wealth Management LLC.

The contents of this book are provided for informational purposes only and are not intended to serve as the basis for any financial decisions. Any tax, legal or estate planning information is general in nature. It should not be construed as legal or tax advice. Always consult an attorney or tax professional regarding the applicability of this information to your unique situation.

Information presented is believed to be factual and up-to-date, but we do not guarantee its accuracy, and it should not be regarded as a complete analysis of the subjects discussed. All expressions of opinion are those of the author as of the date of publication and are subject to change. Content should not be construed as personalized investment advice, nor should it be interpreted as an offer to buy or sell any securities mentioned. A financial advisor should be consulted before implementing any of the strategies presented.

Investing involves risk, including the potential loss of principal. No investment strategy can guarantee a profit or protect against loss in periods of declining values. Any references to protection benefits or guaranteed/lifetime income streams generally refer to fixed insurance products, never securities or investment products. Insurance and annuity product guarantees are backed by the financial strength and claims-paying ability of the issuing insurance company.

Rolek Wealth Management LLC is a Registered Investment Advisor. Please visit our website www.rolekretirement.com/disclosures for important disclosures.

CONTENTS

Preface   ix

Introduction   1

1. Lifestyle Planning   7

2. Expense Planning   17

3. Income Planning   27

4. Investment Planning   41

5. Tax Planning   63

6. Health Care Planning   77

7. Estate Planning   91

8. Tying It All Together   101

Helpful Resources   103

Contact Us   107

About the Authors   109

For those who like to learn and for those who like to plan. May this book and the self-assessments included at the end of each chapter help you improve your retirement planning.

PREFACE

I grew up in Easton, Pennsylvania, a small town about 70 miles north of Philadelphia. It's known for being the home of the former heavyweight-boxing champion Larry Holmes, the Crayola Crayon Factory, and great high school wrestling.

I was born into a family of educators. My mom taught elementary school special ed for 25-plus years. My dad is an elementary school gym teacher and a coach. My brother is also a teacher and a coach.

I teach adult education classes about retirement planning at colleges and universities in the Greater Philadelphia area. The classes are generally attended by people ages 50 and above who want to learn how to get things organized heading into retirement. Outside of the classes, I also work with people one-on-one and teach them how to apply what they learn in class to build their own personalized plan for retirement.

This book was created to make the classroom teachings accessible to those who can't attend a class in person. As of today, classes are only conducted about once per month and they are only held in the Greater Philadelphia area. If you are unable to attend a class in person due to location or scheduling, or if you've attended a class in person and want access to the self-assessments that are only found within this book, this is for you.

At the end of each chapter in the book, you'll find a link to a self-assessment. The assessments were built to help readers identify strengths and weaknesses in their own retirement planning as it stands today. There are nine assessments in total and they take about 60 seconds each to complete. Each assessment begins by asking a short series of questions. After responding to each question and clicking submit, the program will automatically review your responses, calculate the results, and instantly display a confidence score. The confidence score will provide you with immediate feedback and will help you identify areas for improvement in your planning.

After completing the book and each of the self-assessments found within it, if you would like to request help with your own retirement planning, I'll describe how to apply for a private consultation in the final chapter.

I want to be clear right up front that this book does not pretend to have all the answers when it comes to retirement planning. However, by reading it diligently and completing the self-assessment at the end of each chapter, you will identify areas for improvement in your planning. If completing this book helps you identify even one item that can ultimately make a positive impact on your retirement, I hope you'll consider it time well spent.

~ Kyle

INTRODUCTION

This book was created to help people who want to improve their retirement planning. Both pre-retirees and those who have recently retired will benefit from reading it. Many hours of live classroom instruction were distilled down to create a single text that's short enough to be easily digestible, yet deep enough to convey the essential teachings from the classes. The short self-assessments included at the end of each chapter will help you identify strengths and weaknesses in your own retirement planning as it stands today. Those who read the book diligently and complete the self-assessments at the end of each chapter will benefit the most from the teachings found within it.

PROBLEMS AND CHALLENGES ADDRESSED IN THIS BOOK

People heading into retirement and those who have recently retired face many of the same common problems and challenges. *"I'm concerned that I'll run out of money." "I don't know if I'm on the right track." "I have investments, but I don't really have a plan for how I'll use them to generate income in retirement." "I don't know how to make the most of Social Security." "I don't know how I'll handle taxes and health care costs." "I don't have an organized, comprehensive plan that I can actually understand."* This book will discuss how to address each of these common problems and challenges.

TOPICS COVERED

The book is organized into seven chapters that correspond with seven key areas of comprehensive retirement planning and an eighth chapter that ties everything together. Following is a list of the topics covered in this book:

Chapter 1 – **Lifestyle Planning:**
- How will you spend your time during retirement?
- How will you avoid boredom and a sense of loss?

Chapter 2 – **Expense Planning:**
- How much will you need to spend per year to live the life you want in retirement?
- How will inflation impact your expenses over time?

Chapter 3 – **Income Planning:**
- How much total annual income will you have coming in each year during retirement?
- How can you make the most of your Social Security benefits?
- If you have a pension, which option should you select?
- How much dividend and interest income will your investments generate each year?
- Will your income meet your expenses?

Chapter 4 – **Investment Planning:**
- Do you have a collection of investments or do you have an investment plan?
- How can you control market risk during retirement?
- How can you control inflation risk during retirement?

- How will you use your investment portfolio to generate income?
- How can you prevent emotions from derailing your investment plan?

Chapter 5 – **Tax Planning:**
- How will you be taxed when you take withdrawals from retirement accounts?
- How will you be taxed on Social Security and pension income?
- How can you build tax-free assets into your retirement plan?
- How can you plan for Required Minimum Distributions (RMDs)?

Chapter 6 – **Health Care Planning:**
- How much should you plan to spend on health care costs in retirement?
- How can you plan for rising health care costs?
- What does Original Medicare cover?
- How can you fill the gaps in Original Medicare coverage?
- How can you plan for long-term care expenses?

Chapter 7 – **Estate Planning:**
- Who will make decisions on your behalf if you become incapacitated?
- What are the downsides of the probate process?
- Which of your assets would go through the probate process as of today?
- How can you strengthen your estate plan?
- How can you leave a legacy that makes a positive impact on the lives of others?

Chapter 8 – **Tying It All Together:**
- How can you apply for a private consultation?

How to Use the Book

When I was writing this book, a quote came to mind from one of my favorite authors, Napoleon Hill, the author of *Think and Grow Rich*:

> "Knowledge is only potential power. It becomes power only when, and if, it is organized into definite plans of action, and directed to a definite end."

Reading this book will help you build knowledge, but as Napoleon Hill said, knowledge is only potential power. Knowledge becomes power only when it's organized into definite plans of action and directed toward a definite end. At the end of each chapter, you'll find two activities to help you organize what you've learned into definite plans of action:

1. **Self-assessments.** The end of each chapter includes a link to a short self-assessment. The self-assessment will ask you a series of questions related to the topics covered in the chapter. After completing the assessment, a confidence score will be displayed. The confidence score will help you identify the strengths and weaknesses in your current retirement planning.
2. **Follow-up items.** After reading each chapter, use the space provided on the final page to write down notes and follow-up items related to the topics covered in that chapter.

Self-Assessment: Before

The following self-assessment will ask you ten questions to help you see where you stand before starting the book. The confidence score displayed at the end of the assessment will provide you with instant feedback. Later, you'll be able to compare this score to your score after completing the book and see how much you've improved:

To access the first self-assessment, enter the web address exactly as it appears here into your browser: **before.rolekretirement.com**

(**Note:** Be sure the web address is entered in your browser *exactly* as it appears above without www., http://, or https://, or any other characters included in the web address line.)

Before confidence score: _____

HOW CAN YOU APPLY FOR A PRIVATE CONSULTATION?

In the final chapter of the book, we'll discuss how to apply for a private consultation. During the consultation, you'll have a chance to request help with your own retirement planning. Read on to learn more.

CHAPTER 1

LIFESTYLE PLANNING

- How will you spend your time during retirement?
- How will you avoid boredom and a sense of loss?

When retirement planning comes to mind, the first questions people usually think about relate to money. Will I have enough? How should I be invested? When should I start Social Security? How do I plan for health care costs? How do taxes work? These important money-related questions deserve a lot of attention.

However, after all the money questions have been answered and retirement day has finally arrived, many people will wake up in the morning, feel out of place, and think to themselves, "Now what?" Retirement planning that focuses solely on money does not necessarily equate to an enjoyable retirement. Failing to plan how you'll spend your time during retirement can result in boredom and a sense of loss, even after you've achieved financial independence. We'll focus the rest of the book on money, but we'll start with lifestyle planning first.

Lifestyle planning is Step 1 of comprehensive retirement planning. How will I maintain a sense of purpose? How will I find meaning? How will I stay connected socially? Such questions often don't get as much attention as the money questions listed earlier, but they might actually be *more* important if the ultimate goal is to really enjoy retirement.

Good lifestyle planning also results in better answers to all the important money questions. For example, if you don't have any idea how you'll spend your time in retirement, how can you possibly know how much you'll spend each year? If you don't know how much you'll spend, how can you know if you'll have enough money? How can you build a sensible investment plan to fund your lifestyle if you don't know what it will cost? The bottom line is that if retirement planning doesn't start with lifestyle planning, it's not legitimate retirement planning.

I'm not sure exactly sure why this step is skipped so often. Maybe it's because people are so busy today that they can't even contemplate what boredom feels like. Maybe it's because people are so used to having to be somewhere at a certain time that they can't contemplate what not having to be anywhere or do anything feels like. Maybe it's because the concept of lifestyle planning didn't matter as much in the past as it does today.

In the past, when people retired, they weren't as healthy as today. They also didn't have anywhere near as long to live. Because retirement used to be shorter and people were often less equipped to do things that provided them with meaning and enjoyment, lifestyle planning didn't matter that much.

Retirement today has real potential to be a new, fulfilling chapter of life. Lifestyle planning helps you identify how you'll find purpose and fulfillment so that you can prepare to make the most of your retirement.

Finding purpose in retirement can be a challenge because, in many ways, it's a new challenge. Why? During the working years, a person's sense of identity is often at least partially derived from what they do for a living.

If a person's profession is a teacher, for example, they may derive a strong sense of who they are in the work they do every day with students in the classroom. With so many demands placed on the workforce today, and so much time spent at work, it's no wonder that a person's identity is often strongly linked to their profession.

Once people reach retirement and they are no longer actively engaged in their profession, their sense of personal identity may be disrupted or lost. When you're retired and no longer actively engaged in your profession, where will your sense of identity come from? Where will your sense of purpose come from? These are questions that effective lifestyle planning helps address.

Maintaining purpose and finding enjoyment in retirement is different than just staying busy. It's about having a reason to get up in the morning that provides you with a continued sense of belonging, fulfillment, and direction. The people who are happiest in retirement are often those who use their talents to make a positive contribution in the lives of others and to give back in some way.

Ed Merck, a retirement columnist for PBS's Next Avenue, wrote a great article on this topic called "5 Tips to Find Meaning and Purpose in Later Life." Merck mentions he began his search for purpose in retirement by making a list of the activities that promoted a sense of well-being within him. I suggest you consider doing the same for your own lifestyle plan. I've included the link to this article and other helpful articles about Lifestyle Planning in the resources section of the book.

Beyond its positive contribution to an enjoyable life in retirement, maintaining a sense of purpose also has significant health benefits. One 2013 study of 1,500 men and women conducted by the Chicago-based Rush University Medical Center's Alzheimer's Disease Center showed people with a sense of purpose experienced a slower onset of cognitive decline such as a loss of memory and critical thinking skills.

The study showed those who had purpose in life demonstrated a 30 percent slower rate of cognitive decline than those who did not. Further, the study found that having purpose reduced the risk of Alzheimer's disease and contributed to a longer, healthier life.[1]

Of course, finding purpose and enjoyment depends largely on personal preferences. We're all wired differently. The key is to know what works for you. Following are some examples that may help you brainstorm ways to find purpose and enjoyment in your own retirement.

1. **Continuing education.** Many universities let retirement-age people in the community attend classes at no cost. Retirement can present a new opportunity for people to pursue a degree they've always wanted but never had the time to get. If continuing education sounds attractive but getting a degree isn't important, people can also choose to attend classes on-demand at many local colleges periodically to keep their mind sharp, share experiences with younger people, and learn about new things. Online classes can also provide good exercise for your mind without the travel. A lifelong commitment to learning is correlated with an overall sense of happiness.

2. **Babysitting within the family.** As kids leave the nest and start building their own families, I often hear people say they don't get to see their grandkids enough. At the same time, babysitting can be a major expense for young and growing families. Some people in retirement may consider using this as leverage to get to spend more time with the grandkids. When it's convenient, you babysit the grandkids at no cost, which saves your kids money on babysitting and means your grandkids get to spend more time with their grandparents too. Win-win-win.

---

[1] Diane Cole. *Wall Street Journal.* Jan. 13, 2013. "Why You Need to Find a Mission." https://www.wsj.com/articles/SB10001424127887323316804578163501792318298.

3. **Babysitting outside the family.** Some people really like being around kids, while others move to senior communities to get away from kids. If spending time with children on a regular basis is something you enjoy, part-time babysitting may be worth exploring further. Websites like Care.com are specifically designed to connect parents with qualified babysitters. You post a resume, parents may contact you to babysit their kids, and you can choose to accept the offers that are convenient for you. Babysitting can also add some extra spending money to your budget in retirement.

4. **Health and fitness classes.** When people see how expensive health insurance can be in retirement, the motivation to live a healthy lifestyle usually increases. Some people may start the day with an outdoor walk to feel the fresh air, eat some breakfast, and then head over to the gym to take a class. In many ways, exercise can serve the dual purposes of staying healthy and also staying connected socially. Many studies point out that people who exercise regularly are happier too.

5. **Freelance work.** There are many freelance work opportunities available for people in retirement today. Websites such as Upwork.com and Freelancer.com feature job postings for temporary, remote work positions. You post a resume, search available jobs online, and apply to positions that are attractive to you. Freelance work can be entertaining, spark creativity, keep your mind sharp, and also provide a cash flow boost.

6. **Religious group volunteer.** Retirement sparks an increased interest in spirituality for many people. Local religious groups often have a variety of volunteer options available on a consistent basis. Whether it's spending an extra hour or two during the weekend at religious services, teaching religion to youth, or preparing meals for the less fortunate, this type of volunteer work can contribute to a fulfilling retirement experience.

7. **Youth group volunteer.** The Boys & Girls Club of America and the Boy Scouts and Girl Scouts are large organizations that provide turnkey volunteer opportunities to help young people. Local schools are another source of volunteer opportunities related to helping youth. Sharing knowledge and experience with young people can be mutually rewarding and energizing.

8. **Relocating to a new community.** Some people plan to stay in their community during retirement, while others seek the adventure of going somewhere new, either seasonally or permanently. Relocating may be driven by various factors such as weather, cost of living, moving closer to family, or all of the above. On the East Coast, I see the Carolinas becoming more and more popular as a retirement destination due in part to the temperate climate and low cost of living.

9. **Hobby classes.** With more free time, retirement provides a chance to try new things. Classes can be a great way to learn new hobbies. From cooking classes to painting-and-wine nights to pottery classes, there are many possibilities to spark new interests while having fun. Websites like Eventbrite.com provide directories of local classes in many areas throughout the country.

10. **Lyft or Uber driver.** Ride-sharing applications used to be reserved for young people in major metro areas. Now, people of all ages use ride-sharing applications, and they are prevalent in many areas beyond the major metros. Driving for ride-sharing companies can provide retirees with a way to meet new people, a flexible schedule, and extra cash flow. I've heard Uber drivers remark on numerous occasions that they think of their driving time as their "therapy" for the day. For someone who enjoys meeting new people, this can provide a way to meet a variety of people for relatively short stints of time. If you make a bond, maybe a new friendship starts from there. If not, they'll be out of your car soon enough.

Here's a specific example of finding purpose and enjoyment in retirement: My mom recently retired after a long career teaching special education to elementary school students. She's always had a passion for helping children, but the administrative side of the formal teaching role was becoming a challenge.

When she initially retired, she relaxed for a few months. After a few months of taking it easy, she started actively looking at what to do next. I am not sure if her itch to find activities was born out of boredom, or if it was thanks to pestering from my dad (who is still working) that spurred her on, but she didn't sit idle for long.

She ended up posting her resume on Care.com, a website designed to connect qualified babysitters with people who need babysitting. She now babysits several children for families in her local area. Helping children has always been how she finds fulfillment. She found a way to maintain that feeling in retirement.

Successful lifestyle planning for retirement means designing a life around the things that give you fulfillment and enjoyment. As mentioned earlier, successful retirement planning isn't just about money. More money does provide more options, and we'll spend the rest of this book focusing on topics related to money. However, we spent some time up front considering lifestyle planning, and I suggest you do the same for your own retirement.

When you think your lifestyle planning through, you increase the odds that you'll enjoy your retirement. It's no guarantee of happiness, but it reduces the chance that you'll be blindsided by feelings of emptiness and boredom down the road.

SELF-ASSESSMENT: LIFESTYLE PLANNING

Lifestyle planning's role is to determine how you'll maintain a sense of purpose and stay connected during retirement. The self-assessment below will ask you five questions to help you assess where you stand today with Lifestyle Planning. The confidence score displayed at the end of the assessment will provide you with instant feedback.

To access the self-assessment, enter the web address exactly as it appears here into your browser: **lifestyle.rolekretirement.com**

(***Note:*** Be sure the web address is entered in your browser *exactly* as it appears above without www., http://, or https://, or any other characters included in the web address line.)

Lifestyle Planning confidence score: _____

HOW CAN YOU APPLY FOR A PRIVATE CONSULTATION?

In the final chapter of the book, we'll discuss how to apply for a private consultation. During the consultation, you'll have a chance to request help with your own retirement planning. Read on to learn more.

FOLLOW-UP ITEMS

While reading the chapter and taking the self-assessment, did any items come to mind that you think you should follow up on? Use this section to make a note of these.

_____

_____

_____

_____

_____

_____

_____

_____

_____

_____

_____

_____

_____

CHAPTER 2

EXPENSE PLANNING

- How much will you need to spend per year to live the life you want in retirement?
- How will inflation impact your expenses over time?

In the retirement of years past, many people lived relatively sedentary lifestyles. As a result, expense planning wasn't really that big of a deal. Because they weren't very active, people often spent *a lot* less as they got older. Today, however, people are retiring healthier and leading more active lifestyles in retirement. This is largely a very good thing, with one main downside: with all the extra free time, you might actually spend *more* during retirement than you spent while you were working, especially in the early years. This isn't necessarily a bad thing, as long as you plan for it.

Determining how much you'll need to spend each year during retirement to live the lifestyle you want is what Step 2 of comprehensive retirement planning, Expense Planning, addresses. Of course, you do *not* want to skip this step and find yourself running out of money in the middle of your retirement! In this chapter, we'll discuss how to estimate annual expenses in the early years of retirement. We'll also go through an example demonstrating how inflation impacts retirement expenses. Inflation causes prices to increase over time. Because prices *will* increase during retirement and fixed income sources likely *won't*, inflation poses a significant challenge that needs to be addressed with careful planning.

HOW MUCH WILL YOUR RETIREMENT COST, PER YEAR?

Estimating what your annual expenses will be during retirement is the starting point for making many important financial decisions. It's not crucial to have expenses pegged down to the penny, and doing so can be almost impossible anyway. However, it is important to have a ballpark estimate of how much your retirement will cost per year. Retirement expenses will drive important decisions related to Social Security planning, pension planning, investment planning, and other important topics. For example, having an estimate of annual expenses is necessary to answer questions such as:

- When you retire, will Social Security and pension income (if you have one) be enough to cover your expenses each year?
- How much income will you need each year from other sources (such as retirement accounts) to make up the difference between expenses and Social Security?

Common retirement expenses are organized into nine distinct categories below, including comments on how the categories may change in retirement compared to your working years. I've also included an AARP budget worksheet within the resources section of this book that can be used to help estimate your expenses in retirement.

1. **Housing.** This is one of the largest expenses for many US households. However, once the mortgage is gone, this category will decrease. Some housing-related expenses will likely remain throughout retirement, such as property taxes, home maintenance, HOA fees, lawn care, and cleaning services.

2. **Utilities.** Common items in this category include electric, oil and gas, water and sewer, garbage, internet, home phone, and cell phone bills.

3. **Food.** This category includes items such as grocery bills, restaurants, fast food, and coffee. For people who buy lunch every day when they're working, food costs may go down in retirement. For others who will eat out more often when they're retired and have more free time, food costs may go up.

4. **Transportation.** Car payments, car insurance, car repairs, parking fees, fuel costs, public transportation fees, and tolls fit in this category. Without having the commute to work, this category may decrease in retirement. On the other hand, for people who spend more time running errands in retirement than they did commuting to work, this category may increase.

5. **Appearance.** Expenses in this category may include clothing, hair care and other personal care, and dry cleaning. In some cases, no longer needing to dress up for work may decrease clothing costs. In other cases, more time for shopping and personal care may cause appearance-related expenses to increase in retirement.

6. **Entertainment.** Travel, event tickets, club membership fees and dues, fitness club memberships, and other expenses related to entertainment and activities fit in this category. This category may increase, especially during the early years of retirement while people are young, healthy, and active.

7. **Income taxes.** Income from Social Security, pensions, investments, retirement account withdrawals, and part-time work may all be taxable in retirement. (We'll discuss taxes in more detail in Chapter 5.)

8. **Health care.** Health insurance, prescriptions, and out-of-pocket medical costs will be a major expense in retirement. According to the HealthView Services "2017 Retirement Health Care Cost Data Report," the average total annual health care expenses for a 65-year-old couple retiring today is $11,369.

Depending on health conditions and the need for long-term care, these costs can increase dramatically. (We'll discuss planning for health care costs in more detail in Chapter 6.)

9. **Other.** Charitable donations, business-related expenses, alimony, debt service and other items not captured above fit into this category.

HOW WILL INFLATION IMPACT YOUR EXPENSES?

Expenses are likely to increase during retirement as a result of inflation. The following example compares the prices of a new house, a gallon of milk, and a gallon of gasoline in 1987 versus 2017.

Prices in 1987:

- New house: $117,000[2]
- Gallon of milk: $1.07[3]
- Gallon of gasoline: $0.90[4]

Prices in 2017:

- New house: $318,700[5]
- Gallon of milk: $2.39[6]
- Gallon of gasoline: $2.53[7]

---

[2] Census.gov. 2018. "Median and Average Sales Prices of New Homes Sold in United States." https://www.census.gov/construction/nrs/pdf/uspricemon.pdf.

[3] Maryalene LaPonsie. MSN. Aug. 16, 2017. "This is What Milk Cost the Year You Were Born." https://www.msn.com/en-us/money/spendingandborrowing/this-is-what-milk-cost-the-year-you-were-born/ss-AAqcals#image=29.

[4] Office of Energy Efficiency & Renewable Energy. March 7, 2016. "Fact #915: March 7, 2016 Average Historical Annual Gasoline Pump Price, 1929-2015." https://www.energy.gov/eere/vehicles/fact-915-march-7-2016-average-historical-annual-gasoline-pump-price-1929-2015.

[5] Census.gov. 2018. "Median and Average Sales Prices of New Homes Sold in United States." https://www.census.gov/construction/nrs/pdf/uspricemon.pdf.

[6] USDA. March 30, 2018. "National Retail Report-Dairy." https://www.ams.usda.gov/mnreports/dybretail.pdf.

A gallon of milk more than doubled in price, and a house almost tripled! As you can see, when given time to work, inflation has a big impact on prices. With people retiring sooner and living longer today, retirement may last 30 years or more in some cases. That's a long time for inflation to work, and your retirement planning needs to be built to account for substantial price increases over time as a result of inflation.

Inflation is a bigger threat in retirement than it is during working years. Although prices increase while you're working, wages and earnings generally increase too. However, in retirement, key income sources may not increase to keep pace with inflation at all. Pensions (if you still have one) very rarely increase with inflation. Social Security currently includes a cost of living adjustment, but that may go away in the future. As a result, inflation is a threat to long-term retirement security that needs to be addressed by careful planning.

Over the long term, between 1913 and 2017, inflation has increased by about 3 percent per year on average.[8] The following table shows the impact that 3 percent inflation would have on $80,000 per year of retirement expenses over time.

Expense Increases Due to 3% Inflation			
Retirement Year	Annual Expenses	Retirement Year	Annual Expenses
Year 1	$80,000	Year 16	$124,637
Year 2	$82,400	Year 17	$128,377
Year 3	$84,872	Year 18	$132,228
Year 4	$87,418	Year 19	$136,195
Year 5	$90,041	Year 20	$140,280
Year 6	$92,742	Year 21	$144,489

[7] US energy Information Administration. 2017. "Weekly Retail Gasoline and Diesel Prices." https://www.eia.gov/dnav/pet/pet_pri_gnd_dcus_nus_a.htm.

[8] Bureau of Labor Statistics. 2017. "Consumer Price Index." https://www.bls.gov/cpi/.

Year 7	$95,524	Year 22	$148,824
Year 8	$98,390	Year 23	$153,288
Year 9	$101,342	Year 24	$157,887
Year 10	$104,382	Year 25	$162,624
Year 11	$107,513	Year 26	$167,502
Year 12	$110,739	Year 27	$172,527
Year 13	$114,061	Year 28	$177,703
Year 14	$117,483	Year 29	$183,034
Year 15	$121,007	Year 30	$188,525

- In 5 years, $90,041 will be needed to buy what $80,000 bought initially in retirement. Retirement got **$10,041 more expensive in the first 5 years!**
- In 10 years, **$104,382** will be needed to buy what $80,000 bought initially in retirement. Retirement got **$24,382 more expensive in 10 years.**
- In 20 years, **$140,280** will be needed to buy what $80,000 bought initially in retirement. Retirement got **$60,280 more expensive in 20 years.**
- In 30 years, **$188,525** will be needed to buy what $80,000 bought initially in retirement. Retirement got **$108,525 more expensive in 30 years.**

You may be thinking, "I probably won't be able to do anywhere near as much 10 or 20 years down the road, so how much does inflation really matter?" While that's true in many cases, I regularly hear stories today from clients in their 60s with parents in there 90s still living on their own, still driving, still doing yard work, and still riding the exercise bike every day. And that's today. By the time someone in there 60s today reaches 90, who knows what's possible? Assuming you'll slow down too soon is risky.

In addition to that, while some expense will go down later in retirement, such as travel, others may go up, such as health care.

When it comes to health care cost, spending less later on in retirement to make up for poor planning that didn't account for inflation may not be choice. For a single person with no survivors, spending down all their money on health care costs to the point where they become eligible for Medicaid might not be that big of a deal to them. For a married couple, the surviving spouse whose left with nothing may not feel the same way. The point is, don't discount the importance of planning for inflation because you're banking on spending a lot less later on in retirement.

According to HealthView Insights, health care costs have inflated at a rate above 6 percent over the past 50 years, and they are expected to continue their rapid increase into the future[9]. As health care becomes a larger portion of annual expenses in retirement, more of your expenses may experience annual price increases of 6 percent or higher, well above the 3 percent used in the previous example. As a result, retirement expenses may actually increase more substantially over time than the example in the previous chart illustrates. The bottom line is that inflation is a big deal, and it's often overlooked. I've included an inflation calculator in the resources section of the book. You can use it to help you see how inflation can impact your specific level of expenses over time.

HOW CAN YOU PLAN FOR INFLATION?

Effective planning can help prevent you from getting blindsided by inflation down the road. It's important to establish an investment plan that contains some component of growth potential to help combat inflation. (We'll discuss this in more detail in Chapter 4 of this book.)

---

[9] HealthView Services. June 12, 2017. "2017 Retirement Health Care Costs Data Report." http://www.hvsfinancial.com/2017/06/12/2017-retirement-health-care-costs-data-report/.

SELF-ASSESSMENT: EXPENSE PLANNING

Expense planning's role is to determine how much you'll need to spend per year to live the life you want in retirement, factoring in inflation, taxes, health care costs, and other items that may come up along the way. The following self-assessment will ask you five questions to help you assess where you stand today with Expense Planning. The confidence score displayed at the end of the assessment will provide you with instant feedback.

To access the self-assessment, enter the web address exactly as it appears here into your browser: **expense.rolekretirement.com**

(**Note:** Be sure the web address is entered in your browser *exactly* as it appears above without www., http://, or https://, or any other characters included in the web address line.)

Expense Planning confidence score: _____

HOW CAN YOU APPLY FOR A PRIVATE CONSULTATION?

In the final chapter of the book, we'll discuss how to apply for a private consultation. During the consultation, you'll have a chance to request help with your own retirement planning. Read on to learn more.

FOLLOW-UP ITEMS

While reading the chapter and taking the self-assessment, did any items come to mind that you think you should follow up on? Use this section to make a note of these.

_____

_____

_____

_____

_____

_____

_____

_____

_____

_____

_____

_____

CHAPTER 3

INCOME PLANNING

- How much total annual income will you have coming in each year during retirement?
- How can you make the most of your Social Security benefits?
- If you have a pension, which option should you select?
- How much dividend and interest income will your investments generate each year?
- Will your income meet your expenses?

How much total annual income will you have coming in each year during retirement from Social Security and pensions (if applicable)? Will you also have income from other sources, such as part-time work, to supplement Social Security and pensions? Income planning helps identify how much total annual income you can expect to have each year during retirement without needing to start spending down bank accounts, selling investments, and withdrawing principal from your retirement accounts. The primary sources of retirement income that we'll discuss during this chapter are Social Security, pensions, dividend and interest income, and part-time employment.

SOCIAL SECURITY

The Social Security Act of 1935 created the Social Security program to help provide Americans with supplemental retirement income. The program is funded primarily through payroll taxes. Back in 1935 when the program was initiated, there were about 42 workers per Social Security beneficiary. Today, there are less than three workers per Social Security beneficiary. Those demographic shifts are a major reason why the program is facing reforms in the future that may impact retirement benefits.

Currently, benefits are calculated using a formula that factors in your 35 highest-earning years. If you haven't worked for 35 years, years you didn't work will be replaced with zeros in the formula. Benefit estimates are available online after signing up for an account on the Social Security Administration's website, http://www.ssa.gov/myaccount. Paper statements are currently only mailed to people older than age 60 who do not have an account online and are not yet receiving benefits.

A Social Security benefit statement shows an estimate for your retirement benefits if they are claimed at age 62, at full retirement age (this varies between age 65 and age 67 currently, depending on your year of birth—more information is available at ssa.gov), and at age 70. Benefits can be started as early as age 62. However, as an individual delays claiming benefits, the benefit amount will increase by 8 percent per year, or 0.66% per month, up until age 70.

Once you reach age 70, there is no further increase in your benefits. However, Social Security benefits do not start automatically at age 70. You still must go file for them. I have seen examples where people are past age 70 and have not started benefits yet. Don't do that. You're leaving money on the table each month you wait to start your benefits past age 70. The following hypothetical example shows how much Mary's monthly retirement benefit amount increases as it's delayed.

- Mary's Social Security retirement benefit if she starts collecting at age 62: **$2,153 per month**
- Mary's Social Security retirement benefit if she starts collecting at age 66, her full retirement age: **$2,687 per month**
- Mary's Social Security retirement benefit if she starts collecting at age 70: **$3,538 per month**

Starting benefits early means Mary will receive more payments, but they will be smaller. Delaying benefits means that Mary will receive fewer payments, but each check will be larger. The illustration below shows how much Mary would receive in benefits over the course of her life, assuming she lives until age 90.

If Mary starts benefits at age 62:
- Benefit amount: $2,153 per month
- Number of payments received over her lifetime: 336 (28 years × 12 months)
- Total amount of benefits paid: **$723,408** (not including inflation adjustments)

If Mary starts benefits at age 66:
- Benefit amount: $2,687 per month
- Number of payments received over her lifetime: 288 (24 years × 12 months)
- Total amount of benefits paid: **$773,856** (not including inflation adjustments)

If Mary starts benefits at age 70:
- Benefit amount: $3,538 per month
- Number of payments received over her lifetime: 240 (20 years × 12 months)
- Total amount of benefits paid: **$849,120** (not including inflation adjustments)

In this example and using these assumptions, it appears Mary will receive the largest amount of Social Security retirement benefits over her lifetime by delaying benefits until age 70. However, this doesn't necessarily mean that delaying benefits until 70 is the best option in all cases.

Reasons to delay benefits:
- You don't need the money yet.
- To receive a larger Social Security monthly payment amount for life.
- For married couples, delaying benefits may result in a larger survivor's benefit. When the first spouse passes away, the survivor may continue to receive their own retirement benefit, or switch to an amount equal to their deceased spouse's retirement benefit, whichever is higher. Delaying your benefits increases your monthly retirement benefit for your life and may also provide your spouse with a higher benefit after you die too. For more details, see www.ssa.gov/survivors/.
- To avoid earnings penalties. If you claim retirement benefits before your full retirement age and you earn over $16,920 per year (as of 2017), $1 of Social Security benefits are reduced for every $2 that you earn above that limit. (Once you reach full retirement age, however, there is no longer an earnings penalty.) Because of the earnings penalty, if you are still working, it often makes sense to delay benefits until at least your full retirement age.

Reasons to start benefits:
- You need the money.
- To delay touching retirement accounts and other invest-ments until later on in retirement. For example, receiving Social Security income may enable someone to withdraw

less from retirement accounts, or even avoid touching these accounts altogether, until further down the line.

- A limited life expectancy.

Comprehensive retirement planning includes a detailed analysis comparing Social Security filing strategies available in your unique situation to help you get the most from your benefits.

SOCIAL SECURITY SPOUSAL BENEFITS

When both spouses have worked for about the same amount of time and have earned about the same level of income throughout their careers, this strategy won't apply. However, when one spouse has earned significantly less than the other, it can make sense for the spouse with the lower earnings record to claim spousal benefits instead of their own retirement benefit. Here's an example of how spousal benefits work:

- Mary's retirement benefit is $2,600 per month at her full retirement age.
- Jim's retirement benefit is $800 per month at his full retirement age.
- Because Jim's retirement benefit is significantly less than Mary's, he may opt to take the spousal benefit at his full retirement age instead of this own retirement benefit. The spousal benefit entitles him to income equal to half of Mary's full retirement benefit, or $1,300 per month. This does not impact Mary's benefit at all.
- Because the $1,300 per month spousal benefit is higher than his $800 per month retirement benefit, Jim decides to file for the spousal benefit.
- This results in an extra $500 of income per month, or $6,000 extra per year. If Jim lives for 25 years while receiving this benefit, this filing strategy will add $150,000

of additional income to Jim and Mary's retirement, not counting cost of living adjustments.

In this example, an effective filing strategy made a substantial difference over the course of a long term. In this case, it may have meant an enjoyable retirement instead of a struggle. Comprehensive retirement planning helps identify when strategies such as this one can add additional monthly income to the bottom line.

For people who are divorced and not remarried, they may be eligible to receive spousal benefits as described in the example above on an ex-spouse's record. To be eligible, the filer must be at least age 62, the marriage to the ex-spouse must have lasted for at least 10 years, and the filer can't be remarried.

SOCIAL SECURITY SURVIVOR BENEFITS

When one spouse dies, the surviving spouse can elect to continue to receive their own retirement benefit or switch to the survivor's benefit. Here's an example to illustrate how survivor benefits work:

- Mary's retirement benefit is $2,500 per month.
- Jim's retirement benefit is $1,500 per month.
- After both Jim and Mary have reached full retirement age, Mary dies.
- Jim goes to the Social Security office and tells them he wants to switch from receiving his retirement benefit to the survivor's benefit. He'll need to bring a death certificate with him.
- Jim's survivor's benefit in this example will be equal to Mary's retirement benefit, or $2,500 per month.
- Once Jim begins receiving the survivor's benefit, he will stop receiving his own retirement benefit of $1,500 per month.

One reason to consider delaying Social Security benefits is to protect the surviving spouse. For example, if Mary had decided to delay starting her retirement benefit and that delay resulted in her retirement benefit growing from $2,500 per month to $3,500 per month, when Mary died, Jim's survivor benefit would have been $3,500 per month instead of $2,500 per month.

SOCIAL SECURITY BENEFIT TAXATION

Social Security benefits may be taxable depending on your level of income. See Chapter 5 of this book for further discussion about Social Security taxation. The Social Security Administration's website also has additional information:
http://www.ssa.gov/planners/taxes.html.

PENSIONS

Employer-provided pensions are becoming more and more rare. For people who still do have pensions, understanding all of the available options can be a challenge. Because pension decisions are usually irrevocable, it's important to get this decision right the first time. You can't go back and change your mind later. Some employers offer more options than others. Here's a list of common pension options:

1. **Single life.** This option provides income for the life of the employee only. It stops at the employee's death. The income amount will be higher than the joint and survivor options.
2. **Joint and 100% survivor.** This option provides income for the life of the employee and the employee's spouse. The income amount will be unchanged when the first spouse dies. The income amount will be lower than the single life option.
3. **Joint and 100% survivor with pop-up.** This option provides income for the life of the employee and the employee's spouse. However, if the employee's spouse dies

first, the income amount will increase, or "pop-up," to the single life amount. Not all pensions provide this option.

4. **Joint and 50% survivor.** This option provides income for the life of the employee and the employee's spouse. However, if the employee dies first, the income the spouse receives will be reduced by 50%.

5. **10-year period certain.** This option provides income for a 10-year period only. This option's income amount will usually be the highest because it covers the shortest time period.

6. **Lump sum.** This option provides a one-time payout that can usually be rolled over to a Traditional IRA and invested.

Let's use an example. Joe has a pension available through his employer. Here are the options Joe has available:

	Monthly income for Joe	Monthly income for Mary
Single life	$2,000	$0
Joint & 100% survivor	$1,500	$1,500
Joint & 100% survivor with pop-up	$1,450 (Increases to $2,000 if spouse dies first)	$1,450
Joint & 50% survivor	$1,800	$900
10-year period certain	$2,500 for 10 years only	
Lump sum	$500,000 one-time payment to traditional IRA	

What if Joe wants the largest monthly paycheck?

The single life option ($2,000 per month) will give Joe the highest monthly income. However, if Joe dies before his wife Mary, Mary will receive $0. Selecting the single life option can put the surviving spouse at risk.

What if Joe wants fixed lifetime income, and wants the same income to continue to his wife Mary if he dies first?

Either the joint and 100% survivor option ($1,500 per month) or joint and 100% survivor with pop-up ($1,450 per month) will best accomplish Joe's goals. If Joe dies first, both options will provide unchanged monthly income for Mary's life too. If Joe selects the joint and 100% survivor option *without* the pop-up provision and Mary dies first, then Joe's income will stay at $1,500 per month. If Joe chooses the option *with* the pop-up provision and Mary dies first, then Joe's income will pop-up from $1,450 per month to $2,000 per month, which is the option he would have received if he selected the single life pension option.

What if Joe wants to take the money from the pension and invest it in his own Traditional IRA?

The lump sum option will allow Joe to receive a one-time rollover payment into a Traditional IRA in the amount of $500,000. As long as the rollover is processed correctly, tax will not be due at the time of the rollover. In this example, after receiving this one-time payment, Joe will not receive any further payments from the pension.

How should Joe decide between the lifetime income options and the lump sum rollover?

Joe must consider the pros and cons of the lifetime income options versus the lump sum. First, here are the pros and cons of the lifetime income options:

- **Pros:** Consistent lifetime income without having to handle the investing.
- **Cons:** Inflexible, usually doesn't adjust for inflation, usually leaves nothing for beneficiaries after both spouses die.

Second, here are pros and cons of the lump sum option:

- **Pros:** Flexible investment options, growth potential to help protect from inflation, can access the lump sum if needed, can pass the remainder to beneficiaries after both spouses die.
- **Cons:** Exposure to investment risk, may be depleted before life ends.

Help with analyzing the various pension options available and selecting an option appropriate for your situation is an important part of comprehensive retirement planning when a pension exists.

DIVIDEND AND INTEREST INCOME

An investment portfolio can be used to provide additional retirement income without having to sell investments. While accumulating assets in accounts like 401(k)s, 403(b)s, IRAs and brokerage accounts during your working life, the dividends and interest that the investments generate are usually configured to be automatically reinvested. Automatic reinvesting helps the investment portfolio grow over time. However, if supplement income is needed in retirement, the dividends and interest can be paid out instead.

As a hypothetical example, if a $500,000 investment portfolio generated dividend and interest income throughout the year that was equal to about three percent of the portfolio's total value, that would be another $15,000 of income that year, without needing to sell any investments or draw down the account's principal.

Dividends and interest can play an important role in retirement income planning.

To get an idea of how much income your current portfolio may generate, most investment statements will list the amount of dividend and interest income generated throughout the year, even if it's currently being reinvested. By looking at a year-end statement, you may be able to see the total income generated over a 12-month period.

Investment planning, including how dividend and interest income fit within an overall investment plan for retirement, will be covered in more detail in Chapter 4.

Part-Time Employment

Part-time work in retirement is very common today, both to stay active and to earn additional income. There are many ways to make some extra spending money in retirement while having fun and staying active too. Here are some examples:

1. **Reduced workload within the current company.** Some companies offer packages to help experienced workers phase-in to retirement by transitioning to a reduced workload. This usually results in a more flexible schedule. Maintaining health benefits can be very attractive too.

2. **Consulting.** Flexible consulting positions may provide a route to apply the knowledge and expertise you've worked hard to build throughout your career.

3. **Uber or Lyft driver.** Ride-sharing applications provide fully flexible schedules and some element of social interaction.

4. **Paid babysitting.** Care.com and Indeed.com are two sources to find babysitting jobs in your area.

5. **Dog walking or pet sitting.** For people who like animals, an online search for dog walking or pet-sitting positions in your area may result in finding a match.

6. **Tour guides.** Museums, local tourism centers, and national parks can provide a list of open positions in your area.

7. **Sporting events or concerts.** Attend a baseball game and you may notice that many of the workers are retirees who've discovered how to get paid to be at the game. Part-time, seasonal positions are often available to work at events that you might have attended for fun anyway.

8. **Seasonal work at an amusement park.** Working at an amusement park can provide social interaction in a fun environment.

9. **Substitute teacher or teacher's aide.** Many substitute-teaching positions do not require a degree in education. School districts in your area can provide more information about openings.

10. **Golf course employee.** This may be a smart financial move in two ways: income from part-time work, and reduced expenses if the position comes with free greens fees.

WILL YOUR INCOME MEET YOUR EXPENSES?

Will you have enough income coming in to meet your expenses each year in retirement? Or will you need to start drawing down your savings accounts, selling investments, and pulling principal out of retirement accounts right away?

John and Jane are retiring next year at age 66. They look at their Social Security statements and determine they'll receive about $2,500 per month each at their Social Security full retirement age. This is $60,000 per year in total that they'll receive from Social Security. They also have $10,000 per year coming in from a pension. Their total income, before having to dip into any of their accounts is $70,000 per year.

They look at their expenses and determine they'll need about $80,000 per year to live the life they want in retirement. That $80,000 will go up a each year with inflation. Comparing their

$80,000 of expenses to $70,000 of income, they see they'll need to get another $10,000 from somewhere, and probably a little bit more in future years as inflation continues increasing their expenses. Using Step 4 of comprehensive retirement planning, Investment Planning, they'll set up an investment plan to generate the income they need in a way that's built to last for the long term. (Investment Planning is covered in the next chapter.)

SELF-ASSESSMENT: INCOME PLANNING

Income planning's role is to determine how much total annual income you'll have during retirement. The self-assessment below will ask you five questions to help you assess where you stand today with Income Planning. The confidence score displayed at the end of the assessment will provide you with instant feedback.

To access the self-assessment, enter the web address exactly as it appears here into your browser: **income.rolekretirement.com**

(**Note:** Be sure the web address is entered in your browser *exactly* as it appears above without www., http://, or https://, or any other characters included in the web address line.)

Income Planning confidence score: _____

HOW CAN YOU APPLY FOR A PRIVATE CONSULTATION?

In the final chapter of the book, we'll discuss how to apply for a private consultation. During the consultation, you'll have a chance to request help with your own retirement planning. Read on to learn more.

FOLLOW-UP ITEMS

While reading the chapter and taking the self-assessment, did any items come to mind that you think you should follow up on? Use this section to make a note of these.

_____

_____

_____

_____

_____

_____

_____

_____

_____

_____

_____

_____

_____

CHAPTER 4

INVESTMENT PLANNING

- Do you have a collection of investments or do you have an investment plan?
- How can you control market risk during retirement?
- How can you control inflation risk during retirement?
- How will you use your investment portfolio to generate income?
- How can you prevent emotions from derailing your investment plan?

Retirement today can last a long time. With people retiring sooner and living longer, some may spend more time in retirement than they did accumulating assets during their working lives. Because of that, your investment portfolio must be built to last for the long haul.

In the past, when retirement was a relatively short, sedentary time period, investments didn't really need to produce much during retirement. Even if someone chose to put all their money in the mattress after reaching retirement, things may have worked out just fine. Because people weren't living as long and they weren't nearly as active in retirement as they are today, the risk of outliving money was much lower.

Today, however, the demands placed on an investment portfolio during retirement are far higher. Effective retirement planning requires building an investment plan that's fully integrated with the other important aspects of retirement covered in this book. For example, an effective investment plan must be built around other financial resources that will play a role in retirement, such as Social Security and pensions. And it's built to fund the specific amount of expenses incurred each year in retirement, factoring in things like inflation, taxes, and health care costs along the way. Investment Planning is Step 4 of comprehensive retirement planning.

Unfortunately, many people mistake having a collection of investments with having an investment plan for retirement. Having a collection of investments and having an investment plan are two very different things, and failing to realize which one you have can result in exposing yourself to unnecessary risks in retirement.

For example, by the time they reach retirement, a person may have a collection of various IRAs, 401(k) accounts, 403(b) accounts, and other investment accounts. Maybe they chose their investments themselves, or maybe they work with a stockbroker. Although the money is invested, it's not really part of a plan. They haven't figured out how much money they'll need their investment accounts to produce each year to supplement their other income sources, or which accounts they'll take income from first. They haven't factored in inflation, taxes, and rising health care costs in their calculations. There is no plan for how to effectively use Social Security to complement their investments and other income sources. They have successfully collected investments, but it's up to them to figure out how to use them in retirement.

When the investment plan isn't integrated with all of the other important elements of retirement planning, the best-case scenario is that things work out OK but feel unorganized and uncertain along the way. The worst-case scenario is that a risk pops up that completely derails retirement, and this is often caused by something that could have been addressed with effective planning up front.

This isn't a far-fetched hypothetical scenario. This lack of planning is exactly what sent real people in retirement back to work in 2008.

In this chapter, I'll first describe four risks that will impact your money in retirement. Second, we'll use a case study to demonstrate how to use a balanced investment approach to address these four risks. Third, we'll discuss how to protect your investment plan from what's potentially the most damaging risk of all—emotion.

THE FOUR RETIREMENT RISKS

Market Risk. If you're too heavily invested in the stock market when you reach retirement, you may not be able to ride out inevitable market downturns when they come. During your working years, you probably didn't need to touch investment accounts to pay expenses because of your earned income. Because you weren't taking distributions from your accounts yet, when market downturns came, you could ride them out. In retirement, things are different.

After retiring, if you don't plan ahead and are forced to sell investments at bad times to pay expenses, your chance of running out of money goes up. It's important to build an investment plan so that, even in retirement, you have time to ride out market downturns and aren't forced to sell investments at bad times.

Inflation Risk. As we discussed in Chapter 2, inflation increases the cost of goods and services over time. When people only lived for 5 or 10 years in retirement, inflation didn't matter all that much. However, in the 20- or 30-year retirements of today, inflation is likely to substantially increase the cost of goods and services during your retirement.

Especially with the rapid increases in health care costs that are likely to continue into the future, inflation is a risk that needs to be addressed. If inflation is overlooked, rising expenses will slowly eat away at your nest egg, year after year. It's important to deploy your investment portfolio wisely to protect against long-term inflation.

Liquidity risk. When retirement income sources such as Social Security, pensions, and investment income (discussed in Chapter 3) fall short of covering expenses, withdrawing principal from your accounts may be necessary. That's not necessarily bad, but it does require careful planning. Also, at some point during retirement, unexpected expenses such as home repairs or health care costs will pop up, and it's important to plan for this eventuality up front.

For example, if a medical emergency arises, you'll need accessible cash to pay it. If you don't have enough in cash reserves to meet that expense, it could mean having to tap into accounts you didn't plan to touch. This can result in being forced to sell investments at bad times, triggering large tax bills or penalties. An effective investment plan establishes an adequate level of cash reserves so that short-term expenses and emergencies can be covered without disturbing the rest of your plan.

Longevity risk. Because people are living longer and retirement is lasting longer, there's also more time for money to run out. A longer retirement means that inflation has more time to work. It also means there's more time for a severe stock market drop to occur at some point during retirement. These risks don't necessarily need to be disruptive to your retirement at all, as long as they are addressed proactively.

Having scattered investment accounts without a real plan may have worked fine before. However, in today's world, establishing a comprehensive investment plan, not just collecting investment accounts, is essential. Careful planning gives you the best chance to avoid running out of money in retirement.

THE THREE BUCKETS FRAMEWORK

The three buckets are a simple framework that can be used to create an effective investment plan for retirement. Assets are divided into three distinct buckets, and each bucket has a clear purpose. The result is a balanced investment plan that protects against each of the four retirement risks.

The Short-Term Bucket. The short-term bucket's purpose is to protect from liquidity risk and market risk. Money in the short-term bucket should be kept safe and easily accessible. Example products and investments include:

- Checking accounts
- Savings accounts
- Money market accounts
- Penalty-free CDs

The Middle Bucket. The middle bucket's purpose is to protect from market risk and keep up with inflation. Money in the middle bucket should be invested conservatively. Example products and investments include:

- US Treasuries
- Stable value funds
- Fixed-accumulation annuities
- Long-term CDs

The Long-Term Bucket. This long-term bucket's purpose is to beat inflation. Money in the long-term bucket should be invested for long-term growth. Example products and investments include:

- Stocks
- Stock funds
- Growth funds
- International funds

Matching Product and Purpose

It's important to use the right product for the right purpose. For the most part, products aren't either inherently good or bad. Their effectiveness is determined by how you use them within the context of your overall investment plan for retirement.

For example, a savings account is great choice for the short-term bucket because it's safe and easily accessible. However, it pays very little interest. While it's a great choice to protect from market risk and liquidity risk, it's a poor choice to protect from inflation risk.

As another example, an S&P 500 index fund is a great choice as part of the long-term bucket because it has historically provided enough growth to beat inflation by a wide margin, as we'll discuss later in this chapter. However, it can experience large losses in short time periods, like in 2008. While it can be a great choice to address inflation risk over the long term, it's a poor choice to protect from market risk in the short term.

The buckets framework helps drive home the point that different financial products serve different purposes. Each type of product plays a different role to help the overall investment plan work as intended. When you use the right product for the right purpose, you can reduce your risk of running out of money. In order for the buckets framework to be effective, you must maintain it with discipline for the long term. Periodic rebalancing works to ensure the allocation between the buckets stays relevant and appropriate over time.

THREE BUCKETS EXAMPLE

Here's a hypothetical example demonstrating how to use the three buckets framework. Before going through the example, it's important to point out that this is a simplified example, purposefully kept simple to illustrate the key principles at work. In reality, deciding how to divide assets between the three buckets, and how to rebalance over time, is a personal decision. Many individual factors need to be considered, including retirement income sources, expenses, appetite for account value fluctuations, taxes, health situation, legacy planning goals, and other personal considerations. Making specific suggestions on how to divide assets between the buckets and how to rebalance them over time is an important part of the ongoing comprehensive retirement planning work I do with clients. In this example, the Smith family had the following financial situation:

- Annual expenses: $80,000
- Annual income from Social Security and a pension: $70,000
- Annual income shortfall (expenses – income): **–$10,000**
- Total savings and investments: $500,000

Initially, Social Security and pension income is expected to leave the Smiths $10,000 per year short of what they'll need to pay their expenses in retirement. And this $10,000 income shortfall is likely to increase each year with inflation. However, the Smiths do have $500,000 saved. This $500,000 can be used to provide additional income each year to fill their shortfall and pay their expenses. The question for the Smith family becomes how to divide the $500,000 between the buckets so that it has best chance to last for the rest of their lives. The objective is to divide the assets between the three buckets in a way that:

- Addresses each of the four risks discussed earlier in the chapter.
- Makes financial sense for their situation.
- Is a plan they feel comfortable sticking with for the long term.

Here's how they decided to divide their money between the three buckets:

- Short-Term Bucket: $50,000
- Middle Bucket: $200,000
- Long-Term Bucket: $250,000

The Smith Family's Three Buckets—Beginning of the Year

The Smiths positioned $50,000 in the short-term bucket because they felt comfortable with this amount of safe and accessible cash in the bank. It helped them sleep at night. They split up the money in this bucket between a checking account and a higher interest money market account. They can access the checking account whenever they wish. The money market takes two or three days to access funds, but it pays much higher interest than the checking account. In this hypothetical example, they expected to earn about 1 percent per year of interest on this money.

The Smiths put $200,000 into the middle bucket to earn more interest than cash while also keeping it protected from stock market risk. This $200,000 was invested in a combination of US Treasuries, a fixed-accumulation annuity, and a stable value fund they had available within their 401(k) account. In this hypothetical example, they expected to average about 4 percent interest per year on this money.

The Smiths put $250,000 into the long-term bucket for growth and inflation protection. The $250,000 was invested in a portfolio of primarily stock index funds. In this hypothetical example, they expected to average a total return of about 8 percent per year on this money over the long-term.

EXAMPLE: USING THE BUCKETS FOR INCOME

Here's how the Smiths used the buckets to fill their $10,000 annual income shortfall without having to deplete their investment principal.

The short-term bucket. Throughout the year, their Social Security and pension checks were deposited into the short-term bucket accounts. In the preceding example, they received about $70,000 in deposits throughout the year from these income sources, and they had about $80,000 of expenses. This left them with a $10,000 annual income shortfall. This shortfall could have meant that this bucket's value decreased from its initial $50,000 amount down to $40,000 throughout the year. However, as a result of effective planning, the Smith's short-term bucket's value remained fairly steady throughout the year. They used investment income from the middle and long-term buckets to meet their income shortfall and replenish the short-term bucket on an ongoing basis.

The middle bucket. In this hypothetical example, the Smith's investments in the middle bucket earned a 4 percent average annual interest rate. Most of this interest was paid on a monthly basis. They configured their accounts so that the interest paid automatically from their middle bucket accounts to their checking account each month. They earned $8,000 of interest over the course of the year (4 percent interest on the bucket's $200,000 value). This $8,000 of interest income deposited into their short-term bucket throughout the year helped fill most of their $10,000 income shortfall.

The long-term bucket. In this hypothetical example, the Smith's investments in the long-term bucket earned a total annual return of 8 percent. Of that 8 percent total return, 6 percent was attributed to capital appreciation, and 2 percent was attributed to dividend income. The 2 percent dividend income was paid on a quarterly basis. They configured their accounts so that the dividend income automatically paid from their long-term bucket to their checking account each quarter. They earned $5,000 of dividend income over the course of the year (2 percent dividend income on the bucket's $250,000 value).

The $5,000 of dividend income from the long-term bucket, combined with the $8,000 of interest income from the middle bucket, meant the Smith family had total investment income of $13,000 that year. This investment income covered their $10,000 income shortfall. As a result, they did not need to draw down on investment principal at all. The total value of the Smith Family's savings actually increased during this year of their retirement. Here's a breakdown of how the Smith's generated income this year:

- Social Security and a pension income: $70,000
- Middle Bucket income: $8,000
- Long-term Bucket income: $5,000
- Total annual income: **$83,000**

- Total annual expenses: **$80,000**
- Annual income surplus or shortfall (+/-): **+$3,000**

EXAMPLE: YEAR-END BUCKET VALUES

The short-term bucket. The short-term bucket started the year at $50,000. At the end of the year, because of their $3,000 income surplus, this bucket's value increased to $53,000.

The middle bucket. The middle bucket started the year at $200,000. Because the interest income was paid to the short-term bucket on a monthly basis but the principal wasn't touched at all, this bucket stayed level at $200,000.

The long-term bucket. The long-term bucket started the year at $250,000. The 2 percent dividend income was paid out, but the bucket also experienced capital appreciation of 6 percent this year. As a result, this bucket's value increased to $265,000 by the end of the year ($250,000 × 1.06). They may choose to leave this $15,000 of growth within the long-term bucket to increase their investment portfolio's growth potential. Or, they may choose to re-distribute the gains among the other buckets to add more stability and liquidity. For clients that I work with, I suggest rebalancing between the buckets on an annual basis.

For the buckets to work effectively over the long term, the plan must be updated periodically. Periodic tune-ups help adjust for uncertain future events such as market performance, changes in interest rates, changes to inflation, changes to expenses and taxes, and the future of the Social Security program.

The Smith's Three Buckets—End of the Year

- Start of year savings and investments: $500,000
- End of year savings and investments: $518,000
- Net change in portfolio value (+/-): **+$18,000**

EXAMPLE: HOW THE SMITH FAMILY'S INVESTMENT PLAN HOLDS UP AGAINST THE FOUR RETIREMENT RISKS

Let's look at how the Smith Family's investment plan holds up against each of the four retirement risks.

Liquidity risk: What happens if an emergency arises and they need cash?

The $50,000 in the short-term bucket at the beginning of the year can reasonably be expected to cover expenses and emergencies that pop-up. Could they encounter an emergency that requires more than $50,000? Yes. However, this amount felt comfortable to this specific family. Some people might sleep better at night with a larger percentage of their money in cash. Others may lose sleep over having money in the bank knowing it probably isn't earning much interest and is losing ground to inflation. Everyone is different, and there is no perfect answer for how much to keep in cash. Financially speaking, I suggest keeping an amount in cash that can be reasonably expected to cover short-term expenses and emergencies that may pop up.

Inflation risk: What happens as inflation continues to increase prices over time?

As we saw during expense planning in Chapter 2, inflation can have a big impact on expenses over time, especially with rising health care costs. The long-term bucket's purpose is to beat inflation. In this example, the family decided to allocate $250,000 to the long-term bucket for growth potential, inflation protection, and current income. They invested this bucket in a portfolio of primarily stock index funds.

As the following table shows, from 1926 to 2016, large company stocks averaged 10 percent per year, small company stocks averaged around 12 percent per year, and inflation averaged around 3 percent per year. These returns assume dividends are reinvested. Over the long term, the stock market beat inflation by a wide margin. Investing the long-term bucket in a broadly diversified portfolio of stocks or stock index funds and limiting the amount of turnover in the portfolio can provide an effective hedge against inflation over the long term.

This is historical performance data for the stock market as a whole. Actual performance can vary widely from these historical statistics. Past performance does not guarantee future results, especially over shorter time periods. Also, because the family in this example is using the dividends as income and not reinvesting them, the returns they earn will be lower than what they would have experienced if dividends were reinvested.

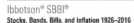

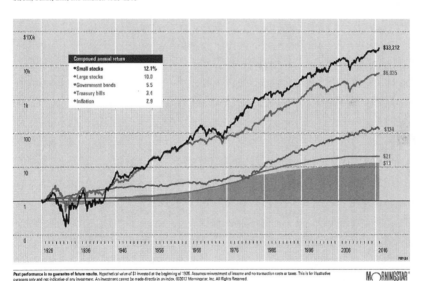

Ibbotson® SBBI®
Stocks, Bonds, Bills, and Inflation 1926–2016

Compound annual return	
• Small stocks	12.1%
• Large stocks	10.0
• Government bonds	5.5
• Treasury bills	3.4
• Inflation	2.9

$33,212
$6,035
$134
$21
$13

Past performance is no guarantee of future results. Hypothetical value of $1 invested at the beginning of 1926. Assumes reinvestment of income and no transaction costs or taxes. This is for illustrative purposes only and not indicative of any investment. An investment cannot be made directly in an index. ©2017 Morningstar, Inc. All Rights Reserved.

MORNINGSTAR®

Market risk: What happens if stock markets drop like in 2008?

Market risk isn't the risk that stock markets go up and down. That's not a risk, it's a certainty. Market risk is being forced to sell at bad times. At some point during the Smith family's retirement, a substantial stock market drop is likely to occur. When that happens, the short-term bucket and the middle bucket will not be expected to lose value. The long-term bucket's value, however, will be expected to decline.

Do they have enough money between their income sources, the short-term bucket, and the middle bucket to ride out these inevitable market downturns? Or will they be forced to sell investments in the long-term bucket to cover expenses?

In this example, the Smith family had an income surplus of about $3,000 per year after realizing investment income from their buckets. With this level of income in comparison to expenses, they may not have to withdraw principal at all from any of their accounts initially. Beyond that point, if they did have to take withdrawals, they have about $50,000 in the short-term bucket and $200,000 in the middle bucket that could be used first before needing to touch money in the long-term bucket.

As a result of the Smith family's effective investment planning, it appears very unlikely that they'd be forced to sell investments in the long-term bucket to cover expenses. Being forced to sell at bad times is exactly what forced people to go back to work in 2008. Effective planning has positioned the Smiths so that they'll have time to ride out the inevitable stock market downturns that will occur at some point during retirement. The Smiths are positioned to maintain growth potential with their investments during retirement to battle inflation, but in a way that's responsible because they are reasonably protected from market risk, the risk of needing to sell at bad times.

The following is an example of why it's so important to have time to ride out stock market downturns in retirement. As shown in the graph, if $100,000 was invested in the stock market in 2007, it would have declined to a low of around $54,689 at the bottom of the stock market downturn in January of 2009.

The Importance of Staying Invested
Ending wealth values after a market decline

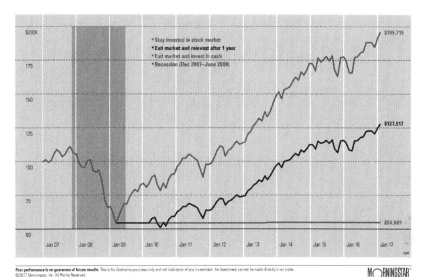

Past performance is no guarantee of future results. This is for illustrative purposes only and not indicative of any investment. An investment cannot be made directly in an index.
©2017 Morningstar, Inc. All Rights Reserved.

However, if they had planned ahead and put themselves in a position where they could ride it out, by around January of 2012, their original $100,000 had been recovered in full. By January 2017, the original $100,000 would have grown to be worth $195,719.

Over the 10-year stretch from 2007 to 2017, the original $100,000 invested in the stock market nearly doubled, even with one of the worst one-year stock market declines in history right at the start of the 10-year stretch. If the person could ride it out, they comfortably beat inflation over this 10-year stretch. If, however, they had to sell investments on the way down to pay expenses because they did not plan effectively, the money may have run out entirely. Strong performance during this 10-year period didn't require any special insights or perfect timing. It just required effective planning so they could ride out the downturn.

As you can probably tell from how many times it's been repeated in this chapter, being able to ride out bad times in the stock market during retirement is essential. As the graph below created by

Morningstar shows, the longer you can go without having to touch the money in your long-term bucket, the less chance you'll have of realizing a loss. Between the years 1926 and 2016, over one-year time periods, the stock market lost value 26 percent of the time. Over five-year time periods, the stock market experienced a loss only 14 percent of the time. Over 15-year time periods, historically speaking during this time period, the stock market has never been down.

This graph is based on past performance and this is not a guarantee of future results. When money is invested in the stock markets, there is always the chance of loss. Also, these statistics show the performance of the stock market as a whole over the long term. If an investment portfolio is highly concentrated within a few individual stocks, or if there is a high level of turnover in the portfolio, results will probably vary widely from the market as a whole. Index funds can be used to closely mimic the performance of stock indexes and provide greater diversification than single-stock investing.

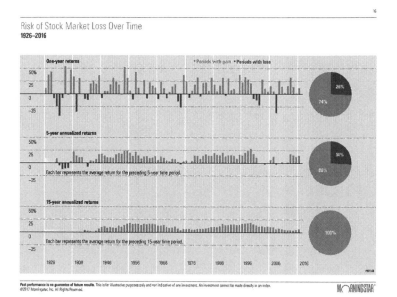

Risk of Stock Market Loss Over Time
1926–2016

Past performance is no guarantee of future results. This is for illustrative purposes only and not indicative of any investment. An investment cannot be made directly in an index.
©2017 Morningstar, Inc. All Rights Reserved.

Longevity risk: What happens if they live a long time?

The risk of running out of money at some point during retirement will always be present, no matter how effective your investment plan is. The future will always have an element of uncertainty. However, effective investment planning can help control and manage risks.

For example, some people are scared that losing money in the stock markets will cause them to run out of money in retirement. We've discussed how to control that risk by giving yourself enough time to ride out inevitable stock market declines. Some people are scared that rising prices and rising health care costs will cause them to run out of money in retirement. We've discussed how to control that risk by maintaining growth potential to battle inflation in a way that's responsible throughout your retirement.

In the example covered in this chapter, by using the three buckets framework, the Smith family has given themselves a reasonable amount of protection from each of the four risks: market risk, inflation risk, liquidity risk and longevity risk. By reviewing their investment plan and making small tune-ups on a periodic basis throughout retirement, they'll remain in control.

Could something pop up during retirement that causes this family to run out of money anyway? Yes. Retirement risks can't be fully eliminated. However, by developing a legitimate, comprehensive investment plan and sticking with that plan for the long term with discipline, they can manage and control risks up to and throughout retirement.

COLLECTING INVESTMENTS VS. INVESTMENT PLANNING

I'd suggest asking yourself whether you have a collection of investments or a legitimate investment plan for your retirement. A collection of investments means that by the time someone is close to retirement age, they've accumulated assets. They may have IRAs,

401ks or 403bs, and other investment accounts. This may have grown to be quite the collection. However, investment planning goes deeper.

For example, do you know how much income you'll need your investment accounts to produce each year to supplement Social Security and any pension income (if you have one)? This can only be answered after completing the first three steps of planning covered in the previous chapters: lifestyle planning, expense planning, and income planning. If you know the answer to this question, that's good. If you don't, it's probably more of a collection of accounts at this stage.

As another example, do you know which account you'll take income from first during retirement? Do you know how you'll take the income? Withdrawals of principal as needed? A fixed monthly amount? Dividends and interest only? A combination of both? If you know the answers to these questions, you may have a good investment plan. If you don't, it's probably more of a collection of accounts at this stage.

If you have a collection of investments, create an investment plan. Planning is an essential step to control and manage risks up to and throughout retirement. We've covered four risks so far. The fifth risk, discussed next, may be the most disruptive. Thankfully, planning can handle this one too.

THE FIFTH RISK: EMOTION

In the preface to the book *The Intelligent Investor,* written by Benjamin Graham, Warren Buffet writes, "To invest successfully does not require a stratospheric IQ, unusual business insights, or inside information. What's needed is a sound intellectual framework for making decisions and the ability to keep emotions from corroding the framework."

Emotions are one of the biggest enemies to sound investment planning for retirement. By retirement age, many people have firsthand experience of the harm that emotions can inflict on investment performance.

Maybe it was buying tech stocks at the top of the bubble in the early 2000s, only to see the investment vanish shortly thereafter. Maybe it was selling investments near the bottom of the stock market's downturn in 2009, then not buying back in because of the fear of making a mistake and painfully watching the dramatic recovery in the markets from the sidelines ever since.

There are many examples in history where investors pour money into stocks at market peaks right before a crash, and then pull money out of stocks at market bottoms, right before the recovery. In retirement, with the stakes so high, reducing the risk that emotions will trigger irrational, short-term decisions with damaging consequences is essential to long-term planning success.

Planning is the deterrent to emotion risk. In the example earlier in the chapter, the Smith family's investment plan helps them see that they'll have a long time to ride out a market downtown when one occurs (see the previous section in this chapter, "Market risk: What happens if stock markets drop like in 2008?" for more details).

They'll still probably feel the natural human emotions associated with market downturns, but they have a framework to protect them from emotional mistakes. They have a written plan to refer to. Ultimately, the plan guards them from making short-term emotional decisions with harmful long-term consequences. The plan helps them ride out market downturns, both financially *and* emotionally.

When another market downturn occurs during retirement, will someone with a collection of accounts who lacks a real investment plan be able to do the same? Maybe, but it will be a lot harder. Why risk it?

SELF-ASSESSMENT: INVESTMENT PLANNING

Investment planning's role is to determine how you will use your investments to generate the income you need to live the lifestyle you want, adjusted for inflation over time. The self-assessment below will ask you five questions to help you assess where you stand today with Investment Planning. The confidence score displayed at the end of the assessment will provide you with instant feedback.

To access the self-assessment, enter the web address exactly as it appears here into your browser: **investment.rolekretirement.com**

(**Note:** Be sure the web address is entered in your browser *exactly* as it appears above without www., http://, or https://, or any other characters included in the web address line.)

Investment Planning confidence score: _____

HOW CAN YOU APPLY FOR A PRIVATE CONSULTATION?

In the final chapter of the book, we'll discuss how to apply for a private consultation. During the consultation, you'll have a chance to request help with your own retirement planning. Read on to learn more.

FOLLOW-UP ITEMS

While reading the chapter and taking the self-assessment, did any items come to mind that you think you should follow up on? Use this section to make a note of these.

_____

_____

_____

_____

_____

_____

_____

_____

_____

_____

_____

_____

CHAPTER 5

TAX PLANNING

- How will you be taxed when you take withdrawals from retirement accounts?
- How will you be taxed on Social Security and pension income?
- How can you build tax-free assets into your retirement plan?
- How can you use Required Minimum Distributions (RMDs)?

No one likes to think about taxes, much less pay them, but proactive tax planning is an important component of retirement planning today. In most cases, the majority of retirement savings are found within accounts that haven't been taxed yet, such as traditional IRA accounts, 401(k) accounts, and 403(b) accounts. In addition to that, key retirement income sources like Social Security and pensions are often taxable in retirement. Because many of the financial resources that retirees rely upon will be taxed throughout retirement, if taxes go up in the future and you don't plan ahead, it can have significant impact on your bottom line. Step 5 of comprehensive retirement planning, Tax Planning, works to ensure that rising future tax rates will not derail your retirement.

For example, if someone has $1 million saved between 401(k) and traditional IRA accounts, they may assume they have $1 million to spend in retirement. However, when taxes are factored in, that $1 million saved won't give them anywhere close to $1 million to spend. Instead, depending on their income, where they live, and what tax rates are in the future, that $1 million saved may only result in around $700,000 or $800,000 of after-tax money they can actually use to pay expenses. If taxes go up, they'll net even less. If they failed to plan and overlooked taxes, they may run out of money much sooner than expected as a result.

In this chapter, we'll cover how taxes will impact retirement accounts and important income sources, such as Social Security and pensions. Next, we'll discuss how to combat the risk of rising future tax rates by building tax-free assets into your plan. Lastly, the government mandates distributions from certain types of retirement accounts beginning at age 70.5. These mandatory distributions are called Required Minimum Distributions (RMDs), and we'll wrap up this chapter by covering that topic.

PRE-TAX RETIREMENT ACCOUNT WITHDRAWALS

When you put money into a retirement account without paying taxes up front, you'll have to pay income tax later when you take the money out. Traditional IRA accounts, pre-tax 401(k) accounts, and pre-tax 403(b) accounts all fit into this category.

For example, if a person takes a $50,000 withdrawal from their traditional IRA account this year, the entire pre-tax amount gets added to their taxable income for the year. In most cases, the entire account balance is pre-tax, so the entire withdrawal is added to their taxable income for the year. In some cases, if a portion of the account is after-tax, a portion of the withdrawal will be excluded from income.

The bottom line is that, once taxes are factored in, a $50,000 withdrawal from a traditional IRA may only net $35,000 or $40,000 of real money after taxes that can be used to pay expenses. Again, $1 million saved in pre-tax retirement accounts results in nowhere near $1 million that can be used to pay expenses. When people fail to consider tax implications, they may mistake the amount they see on paper in their retirement accounts with the amount of real money they'll have to pay expenses in retirement. This can lead people to miscalculate where they stand today and assume they're in a much stronger position than reality.

When you withdraw money from pre-tax retirement accounts, you can have taxes withheld up front to reduce the risk of a big tax surprise when it's time to file. This can be set up to work sort of like how taxes are withheld from your paycheck while you're working. While both federal and state taxes can be withheld, some states do not tax retirement account withdrawals, so it doesn't make sense to withhold state tax in locations where withdrawals aren't taxable at the state level. To find out if your state taxes retirement account withdrawals, visit your state's Department of Revenue website or speak to a qualified local CPA. A CPA can also provide advice on what specific percentage to withhold from your retirement account distributions given your unique tax situation. Withholding too little can result in an unwanted tax surprise when you file, while withholding too much is essentially providing an interest-free loan to the government.

TAX ON RETIREMENT INCOME SOURCES

Many important retirement income sources are also taxable in retirement.

Pensions. Pension income is almost always taxable at the federal level. Depending on where you live, pension income may also be taxable at the state level. Pensions usually allow the recipient to elect a specific percentage of each payment to be withheld for taxes.

For example, if a pension pays an annual income benefit of $50,000 per year and 20 percent is withheld for federal taxes, $40,000 will be the net amount received that year after taxes are taken out.

Social Security. As of 2018, for married filers with *combined income* over $32,000 and for single filers with *combined income* over $25,000, a portion of Social Security benefits will be taxable. Combined income is calculated by adding half of your Social Security benefits to all other income, including tax-exempt interest. Both IRS.gov and SSA.gov publish up-to-date information about how Social Security benefits are taxed and further instructions on how to calculate combined income.

Based on the level of combined income, filers may pay federal income tax on up to 85 percent of their Social Security benefits. For example, if a family has combined annual Social Security benefits of $50,000, then up to $42,500 could be taxable as income at the federal level ($50,000 × 85 percent). Tax treatment at the state level varies. Consult your state's Department of Revenue website or a local CPA for more information about state-specific rules.

Part-time work. Earned income from part-time work will be taxable during retirement. In addition, if Social Security benefits are claimed before full retirement age, earned income may reduce Social Security benefits (discussed more in Chapter 3). However, after obtaining full retirement age, earned income no longer impacts Social Security benefits. The Social Security Department's website ssa.gov publishes and updates rules related to earnings limitations.

Interest income. Most interest income is taxable at ordinary income rates. Common sources of interest income include savings accounts, CDs, bonds, and bond mutual funds. For example, if $10,000 of interest income was earned during the course of the year, that $10,000 of interest is added in with other sources of taxable income, and it's taxed at ordinary income rates. Municipal bonds pay interest income that is tax-free at the federal level, and potentially tax-free at the state level as well.

Dividend income. Qualified dividend income is taxed at a preferred rate below ordinary income. Nonqualified dividend income is taxed at ordinary income rates. IRS.gov publishes and updates specific information about what constitutes a qualified dividend versus a nonqualified dividend, and the specific tax rates that apply to each type of dividend.

When US stocks are held as long-term investments, the dividends received are usually classified as qualified dividends and will usually receive favorable tax treatment. For example, if $10,000 of qualified dividend income is received during the year and is taxed at a qualified dividend rate of 15 percent, then $1,500 would be the tax, and $8,500 would be the net income after taxes. Qualified dividend tax rates vary based on a filer's tax bracket. IRS.gov publishes updated qualified dividend tax rates.

THE IMPACT OF FUTURE TAX RATE INCREASES

During the working years, there's usually more flexibility to adjust to changes in the tax code than during retirement. When taxes go up during retirement, options are limited. As a result, a future tax rate increase can have a major impact on a retiree's bottom line. With a rapidly growing budget deficit and increasing demands placed on government programs like Social Security, Medicare, and Medicaid, a substantial tax increase in the future certainly isn't out of the question.

For example, if a person's effective tax rate is initially 20 percent during retirement, when they withdraw $50,000 from their traditional IRA, $10,000 will go to tax and $40,000 will go in their pocket. However, if their effective tax rate increases to 30 percent at some point during retirement, $15,000 will go to tax and only $35,000 will go in their pocket. In other words, they just got a $5,000 pay cut.

Whether taxes will go up in the future or not is uncertain. However, in many cases, Roth accounts can be built into the comprehensive plan to hedge against future tax rate increases. Because Roth accounts can distribute tax-free income down the road, if taxes do increase later, building Roth now will pay off then.

FOUR WAYS TO BUILD ROTH ASSETS

With Roth accounts, money goes in after-tax, and if requirements are met, money can be withdrawn tax-free. Roth accounts are composed of contributions (the money you put in) and earnings (the return earned on your contributions). Contributions can be withdrawn at any time tax-free. Earnings can come out tax-free if the account owner is above age 59 ½ and has owned the account for at least five years.

The major benefit of Roth accounts is that, when these requirements are met, all future growth can be distributed tax-free. Over the course of a long retirement, this can result in substantial tax-free asset accumulation. Here are four ways to fund Roth accounts:

#1: ROTH IRA

In 2018, individuals above age 50 can contribute the lesser of $6,500 or 100% of earned income to a Roth IRA, if income limitations are met. This $6,500 limit is per person. For married couples, both spouses may be eligible to contribute this $6,500 amount. Even if one spouse is not working, the nonworking spouse may still be eligible to contribute up to $6,500 to their own IRA as long as the working spouse's earned income exceeds $13,000 for the year.

The following table shows the income limits for 2018. Income limits are based on your modified adjusted gross income (MAGI). IRS.gov publishes updated income limits on an annual basis.

A qualified CPA can help with calculating your specific modified adjusted gross income and determining your Roth IRA contribution eligibility.

2018 Roth IRA Limits			
Filing status	Full contributions if income below	Partial contributions if income between	No contribution allowed above
Single	$120,000	$120,000– $135,000	$135,000
Married filing jointly	$189,000	$189,000– $199,000	$199,000

#2: ROTH 401(K) OR ROTH 403(B)

Some employers who offer 401(k) or 403(b) plans allow their employees to make Roth contributions into the plan. If the employee makes Roth contributions, the money goes into the plan after-tax instead of pre-tax. However, when the money is withdrawn down the road, all contributions and future growth come out tax-free. At retirement, the Roth 401(k) or 403(b) can be rolled over to a Roth IRA to maintain the tax-favored status.

There are no income eligibility limits for Roth 401(k) or 403(b) contributions. Because of that, high-income earners who are ineligible to contribute to the Roth IRA may consider using this option to grow Roth assets. In 2018, individuals above age 50 are permitted to make Roth contributions of up to $24,500 per year into 401(k) or 403(b) accounts. IRS.gov publishes updated contribution limits on an annual basis.

#3: AFTER-TAX CONTRIBUTIONS INTO A 401(K) OR 403(B)

Many employers allow additional after-tax contributions into their 401(k) or 403(b) plans. For people above age 50 in 2018, the total contribution limit into a 401(k) and 403(b) account is $55,000, including all employee and employer contributions.

For example, if an employee contributes $24,500 to the 401(k) on a pre-tax basis and the employer does not contribute anything to the plan, that employee may be eligible to contribute an additional $30,500 into their 401(k) account on an after-tax basis. If the employee contributes $24,500 and the employer contributes $10,000, the employee would be able to contribute up to $20,500 after-tax to reach the $55,000 total limit. At retirement, the after-tax portion of the account can then be rolled over into a Roth IRA, without any income restrictions imposed. Earnings accrued on the after-tax contributions are considered pre-tax, and can be rolled over to a traditional IRA at retirement. IRS.gov publishes updated contribution limits on an annual basis.

#4: ROTH CONVERSION

The IRS permits individuals to convert any portion of a traditional IRA to a Roth IRA, without income restrictions. To perform this transaction, the amount converted must be added to the current year's taxable income. For example, if a person converts $100,000 from a traditional IRA to a Roth IRA, they'll have to add an additional $100,000 to their current year's taxable income. As a result, doing large conversions all at once can result in a significant tax bite. Effective planning techniques can help minimize tax implications of Roth conversions.

One planning technique is to perform small conversions over a period of years instead of performing a large conversion all at once. For example, if the person above converts the $100,000 traditional IRA to a Roth IRA by performing a series of smaller, $20,000 conversions over a five-year period instead of converting all $100,000 at once, they will likely save money on taxes.

Another technique is timing conversions for lower-income years. In a situation where a person is close to retirement and their income is expected to drop substantially in retirement, it probably makes sense to wait until retirement to begin conversions. In this scenario, because they will probably be in a lower tax bracket once they retire, waiting to begin conversions will likely save them money on taxes. This scenario is fairly common.

DOES A ROTH MAKE SENSE FOR ME?

Roth accounts don't make sense in all cases. With Roth accounts, there's no tax deduction today, but there are tax-free withdrawals later. With pre-tax accounts, there's a tax deduction today, but there's income tax due later. The question becomes: Is it better to pay the taxes now or later?

Mathematically speaking, here's how the comparison works out:

- If your tax rate is lower when you take withdrawals than it is today, the pre-tax retirement account would have worked out better than Roth.
- If your tax rate is higher when you take withdrawals than it is today, the Roth account would have worked out better than the pre-tax option.
- If your tax rate is about same when you take withdrawals down the road as it is today, the Roth account would have worked out slightly better. Because contribution limits are the same dollar amount for pre-tax accounts and Roth accounts, you're actually saving more for retirement when you save into Roth since the money is already after-tax. Also, because Roth IRAs do not have required minimum distributions (more on these later in this chapter), the full value of the Roth IRA has more time to benefit from compound interest than a traditional IRA.

Comprehensive retirement planning includes an analysis of when and how to build Roth assets into the structure of your overall plan given your unique situation. Just as important as determining when and how to build Roth assets, using Roth wisely will help maximize the benefits of tax-free growth over the course of a long retirement.

USING ROTH ACCOUNTS IN RETIREMENT

In most cases, Roth accounts should be invested as part of the long-term bucket. The long-term bucket has the highest expected long-term rate of return of the three buckets because it's invested for long-term growth. It's beneficial to own investments with the highest expected long-term return in Roth accounts because all of the growth you earn is yours to keep, tax-free. (Refer to Chapter 4 for a more detailed discussion of investment types that fit within the long-term bucket.)

For example, if a traditional IRA grows from $100,000 to $200,000, your money doubled, but so did your tax bill. If a Roth IRA grows from $100,000 to $200,000, all that growth is tax-free. Also, because more time to compound means more growth, it generally makes sense to use Roth assets last in retirement.

REQUIRED MINIMUM DISTRIBUTIONS (RMDS)

Beginning April 1 of the year after a person turns 70 ½, the government requires owners of traditional IRAs, 401(k) accounts, 403(b) accounts, and other qualified retirement plans to take a minimum annual withdrawal from their accounts, called the Required Minimum Distribution (RMD).

The RMD formula begins by calculating the total value of retirement plans for which the distributions are required. For example, if a person has a $500,000 traditional IRA at company No. 1, a $300,000 traditional IRA at company No. 2, and a $200,000 old 401(k) they never rolled over from a previous employer, they would have a total of $1,000,000 in retirement accounts from which minimum distributions are required.

The formula then divides this total value by an age-specific number published in the IRS's Uniform Lifetime Table for RMDs, found on IRS.gov. As of 2018, someone who is age 70 is required to divide the total value of their retirement accounts by 27.4 to calculate their RMD.

- $1,000,000 = Total retirement account value
- 27.4 = Uniform Lifetime Table number
- $36,496 = RMD for the year

The age-specific Uniform Lifetime Table number decreases each year a person ages. This means that the Required Minimum Distribution amount becomes a larger percentage of the total value of all retirement accounts owned by the individual each year as time goes on.

In a situation where a person has multiple retirement accounts, the distribution does not have to come from each individual account. They can choose to take the distribution from any one account, or any combination of the accounts.

If the correct amount is not distributed, there is a tax penalty equal to 50 percent of the amount that was supposed to be distributed but wasn't. Although the first distribution must be taken by April 1 of the year after the year the person turns age 70 ½, all future distributions must be taken by December 31 each year. With such a large tax penalty at stake, it's important to get this right. A qualified CPA can help with calculating the RMD and reporting it correctly.

There are two main exceptions to the RMD rules. First, Roth IRAs do not require minimum distributions. Second, if a person is still working beyond age 70 ½, they aren't required to take minimum distributions from their current employer's retirement plan until after retirement, as long as they are not also an owner of the company. Note that, in this scenario, they still have to take RMDs from other non-Roth retirement accounts they have that aren't through the current employer.

These required annual distributions do not necessarily need to impact the investment plan. For example, Joe is above age 70.5 and has a Traditional IRA that's invested as part of his long-term bucket. He's required to take his RMD each year for tax purposes, but he doesn't necessarily need to use the RMD as income and spend it. If he doesn't need the money as income, the RMD can be distributed into a nonretirement account that's also part of his long-term bucket and is invested in relatively the same way as the Traditional IRA. Taxes can be withheld at the time of the distribution from the Traditional IRA to the nonretirement so that he won't need to disrupt cash in the short-term bucket to pay taxes either.

The bottom line is that although you are required to take money out of retirement accounts at a certain point, good planning can help you retain control over how these distributions are deployed.

Roth IRAs and Required Minimum Distributions

As mentioned earlier in the chapter, unlike traditional IRA accounts, Roth IRAs do not require any minimum distributions during the account owner's lifetime. Not being forced to take annual distributions enhances the power of compound interest over time. Further, if a spouse is named the beneficiary of the Roth IRA, they also do not have to take required minimum distributions during their lifetime as long as they rollover the account into their name. Once someone who is a not a spouse inherits the Roth IRA, annual minimum distributions are required but aren't taxable.

SELF-ASSESSMENT: TAX PLANNING

Tax planning works to ensure that rising future tax rates will not derail your retirement. The self-assessment below will ask you five questions to help you assess where you stand today with Tax Planning. The confidence score displayed at the end of the assessment will provide you with instant feedback.

To access the self-assessment, enter the web address exactly as it appears here into your browser: **tax.rolekretirement.com**

(*Note:* Be sure the web address is entered in your browser *exactly* as it appears above without www., http://, or https://, or any other characters included in the web address line.)

Tax Planning confidence score: _____

HOW CAN YOU APPLY FOR A PRIVATE CONSULTATION?

In the final chapter of the book, we'll discuss how to apply for a private consultation. During the consultation, you'll have a chance to request help with your own retirement planning. Read on to learn more.

FOLLOW-UP ITEMS

While reading the chapter and taking the self-assessment, did any items come to mind that you think you should follow up on? Use this section to make a note of these.

_____

_____

_____

_____

_____

_____

_____

_____

_____

_____

_____

_____

CHAPTER 6

HEALTH CARE PLANNING

- How much should you plan to spend on health care costs in retirement?
- How can you plan for rising health care costs?
- What does Original Medicare cover?
- How can you fill the gaps in Original Medicare coverage?
- How can you plan for long-term care expenses?

How do you handle health care costs once you retire and lose coverage through your employer? Before retirement, health care costs are often an afterthought. After retirement, health care costs are front and center. After years of receiving coverage through an employer, concerns about health care in retirement often stem from a fear of change and a fear of having to figure all this out on your own for the first time. There are some very good health care coverage options available for those age 65+ today. Once people go through Step 6 of comprehensive retirement planning, Health Care Planning, fears around obtaining health care in retirement and planning for costs often begin to subside.

CONSIDERING HEALTH CARE COSTS IN RETIREMENT

According to the 2017 Health Care Costs Data Report created by HealthView Services, the average cost of health care for a 65-year-old retired couple is $11,369 per year, in today's dollars. This average includes costs for Medicare Part B and Part D, a Medicare Supplement Plan, dental insurance and all other out-of-pocket expenses. The cost for that same level of health care services was $10,699 in the 2016 survey, representing a 6.3 percent cost increase year-over-year.[10]

A 65-year-old retired couple today is projected to need a total of $404,253 for health care costs throughout the course of their retirement, in today's dollars. This estimate includes costs for Medicare Part B and Part D, a Medicare Supplement Plan, dental insurance and all other out-of-pocket expenses. Health care costs can vary widely from state to state, and even from county to county within the same state. Your state department's website may post more precise estimates for your specific location.

Although there is no single solution to address rising health care costs, there are a few steps you can take to plan. First, enroll in Medicare Part A and Part B when you are required to do so, and select a cost-effective Medicare Supplement plan. More details on this later in the chapter.

Second, maintain a sound investment plan (Chapter 4) that continues to pursue growth potential during retirement in a way that's responsible. Doing so can help fund rising health care costs down the road.

Third, people who have a High Deductible Health Plan and are not yet enrolled in Medicare may be eligible to contribute to a Health Savings Account (HSA). These accounts allow tax-deductible

---

[10] HealthView Services. June 12, 2017. "2017 Retirement Health Care Costs Data Report." http://www.hvsfinancial.com/2017/06/12/2017-retirement-health-care-costs-data-report/.

contributions *and* tax-free distributions for qualified medical expenses. These are the only accounts I know of today that allow the potential of a tax-deduction on the way in *and* tax-free distributions on the way out. More information about these accounts is available on healthcare.gov. I've also included a link to more information about HSAs in the resources section towards the end of this book.

ORIGINAL MEDICARE

Original Medicare (Part A & Part B) is a health care program managed by the federal government that provides medical coverage for individuals age 65 and above. Those receiving Social Security disability benefits and those with end-stage renal disease may also be eligible to receive benefits through Medicare prior to age 65.

While Part A and Part B do cover many of the health care expenses that you'll incur during retirement, these plans also have significant coverage gaps. In addition to enrolling in Medicare Part A and Part B, you're strongly encouraged to also enroll in either a Medicare Advantage Plan or a Medicare Supplement Plan to fill many of these coverage gaps in a cost-effective way. We'll discuss more details about these plans later in the chapter.

Medicare's initial enrollment period begins three months before turning age 65 and lasts until three months after turning age 65. If you have started receiving Social Security retirement benefits before age 65, in most cases, you will be automatically enrolled in Medicare Part A and Part B effective the month your turn 65.

If you have not started receiving Social Security retirement benefits before age 65, you may be required to enroll in Medicare once you reach 65 on your own. Failure to enroll in Medicare when required to do so can result in a penalty on Medicare Part B premiums for life. Visit Medicare.gov for more information about Medicare enrollment requirements and deadlines. Visit ssa.gov or a local Social Security office in person to enroll in Medicare when required to do so.

Original Medicare includes Medicare Part A and Medicare Part B. The following is an overview of the services covered and the costs involved. You can find more complete and detailed information about services covered and costs at Medicare.gov.

Medicare Part A (hospital insurance). Part A may cover a portion of expenses for services such as:

- Hospital care
- Skilled nursing care
- Hospice care
- Home health care

As of 2018, if you or your spouse paid Medicare taxes for at least 10 years of work, your Part A premium will be $0. Most people receive Medicare Part A at no cost. For those who must pay for Medicare Part A because they do not meet the work history requirements, the premium can be as high as $422 per month as of 2018. It's important to note that the skilled nursing and home health care services Medicare covers are only for the purposes of rehab or temporary services. If you require home health care or skilled nursing care on an ongoing, permanent basis, it will not be covered by Medicare.

Medicare Part B (Medical insurance). Part B may cover a portion of expenses for services such as:

- Clinical research
- Preventive services
- Mental health services
- Medical supplies

As of 2018, monthly premiums for Medicare Part B vary based on income. The standard Part B premium starts at $134 per month, and can more or less depending on your level of income.

Now we'll discuss some of the shortfalls of Medicare Part A and Part B. First, when a service is covered by either Medicare Part A or Part B, you still may be responsible for deductibles, coinsurance and copayments. These costs can add up throughout the course of the year, and they can fluctuate significantly from year to year.

Second, some health care services won't receive any coverage through Medicare A and B. To find out if Medicare covers a specific service that you may need, visit Medicare.gov for more information. Here is a partial list of services that may not receive coverage:

- Most dental care
- Most eye care
- Prescription drugs
- Hearing aids
- Long-term care

Third, another shortfall with Medicare Part A and Part B is that they do not by themselves establish any annual out-of-pocket maximum for health care costs. This means that, if significant health care costs are incurred within a given year, there's no limit to the amount that you may be on the hook to pay personally. This can lead to substantial losses in short time periods. We'll discuss how to address this risk below.

FILLING THE GAPS IN ORIGINAL MEDICARE

When enrolling in Medicare Part A and Part B, you're strongly encouraged to also enroll in either a Medicare Advantage Plan or Medicare Supplement Plan. Both of these plans can be used to fill many of the coverage gaps in Medicare Part A and Part B in a way that's relatively cost effective. We'll cover some important distinctions between Medicare Advantage Plans and Medicare Supplement Plans below. More complete information is available at Medicare.gov.

First, by way of background, Medicare Advantage Plans (also called Medicare Part C) and Medicare Supplement Plans (also called Medigap Plans) are optional insurance plans offered by private insurance companies to fill many of the gaps in Medicare Part A and Part B coverage.

Medicare Advantage Plans (Medicare Part C). Medicare Advantage Plans provide coverage for the services included with Medicare Part A and Part B, as well as additional services such as prescription drugs, vision care, and dental care. Specific services covered and plans available vary from state to state. Medicare.gov has more information about how to find and compare the specific Medicare Advantage Plans available in your area.

Medicare Supplement Plans (Medigap Plans). Medicare Supplement Plans are designed to pay all or most of the out-of-pocket expenses associated with Medicare Part A and Part B, such as copayments, coinsurance, and deductibles. Specific services covered and plans available vary from state to state. Medicare.gov has more information about how to find and compare the specific Medicare Supplement Plans available in your area.

Because individuals aren't permitted to enroll in both a Medicare Advantage Plan and a Medicare Supplement Plan, you must choose between the two options.

In general, Medicare Supplement Plans provide greater flexibility to choose a health care provider than Medicare Advantage Plans. Medicare Advantage Plans usually require use of an in-network provider. Depending on the specific service needed and where you live, that can mean long travel times to get to a provider who is in-network. In contrast, Medicare Supplement Plans generally allow use of any provider who accepts Medicare. This often translates to much greater flexibility and convenience.

Step 6 of comprehensive retirement planning, Health Care Planning, will coach you through the selection process between Medicare Advantage Plans and Medicare Supplement Plans so that you're not left to figure this out on your own.

While Medicare Advantage Plans and Medicare Supplement Plans provide many benefits, neither of these plans covers what may be the most concerning category of health care expenses today: long-term care.

LONG-TERM CARE

If you've had a loved one go to a nursing home, you've likely seen firsthand how long-term care expenses can burn through retirement savings in short order. When there's no plan for how long-term care expenses will be paid, a life savings can be depleted quickly, and a surviving spouse can be left all alone to deal with the aftermath.

In general, long-term care is assistance with basic personal tasks of everyday life for people who can't perform these personal tasks themselves. As a result of increased life expectancy, the need for long-term care is increasing substantially. Unfortunately, so is the cost.

According to longtermcare.acl.gov, someone turning age 65 today has a 70 percent chance of needing some type of long-term care services at some point in the future. Paying for long-term care expenses out of pocket can quickly deplete savings. Costs vary widely from state to state and can run considerably higher in urban areas.[11] National average costs for different levels of long-term care services, according to the 2017 Genworth Cost of Care Survey, are listed below.

---

[11] Genworth. 2017. "2017 Cost of Care Survey." https://www.genworth.com/aging-and-you/finances/cost-of-care.html

- Nursing home cost (private room): $8,121 per month
- Nursing home cost (semi-private room): $7,148 per month
- Home health aide cost: $4,099 per month
- Assisted living facility cost: $3,750 per month

How long might you need long-term care? According to longtermcare.acl.gov:

- The average length of stay in a long-term care facility is 3 years.
- For women, the average length of stay is 3.7 years.
- For men, the average length of stay is 2.2 years.
- About 20% of people will need long-term care services for 5+ years.

As an example, based on the average costs listed above, a three-year stay in a semi-private room would cost $257,328 in today's dollars ($85,776 per year × 3 years). Once inflation is considered, that cost for someone retiring today could be well over half a million dollars by the time long-term care is needed down the road.

Also consider that if you have to pay long-term care costs out of pocket, after-tax money will be needed to cover the expenses. If $428,880 is needed after-tax, that might require withdrawals of $600,000 or more from pre-tax accounts like a traditional IRA or 401(k) once taxes are considered. This can be a major financial burden, not only for the person needing the care but especially for a surviving spouse who may still have many healthy years left and need to continue paying for expenses.

PLANNING FOR LONG-TERM CARE

There are many options to consider when planning for long-term care costs. Comprehensive retirement planning can help with determining which option makes the most sense for your unique situation.

Self-insuring. Paying for long-term care expenses out of pocket is a viable option when the person has accumulated enough resources to do so. However, for married couples, it's important to consider how this will impact a surviving spouse.

Long-term care insurance. Traditional long-term care insurance policies allow an individual to pay premiums to an insurance company in exchange for a tax-free long-term care benefit in the future, if long-term care is needed. The main benefit to this approach is that, for a price, you're able to transfer the risk of paying for some portion of long-term care expenses to an insurance company. However, there are also two main downsides to consider.

First, if you don't need long-term care, in most cases the premiums are lost. Second, insurance companies usually reserve the right to raise premiums on active policyholders in the future, and many have done so. With the rising costs of long-term care, it's likely that premiums will continue to go up in the future. Longtermcare.acl.gov has additional information about long-term care insurance.

Long-term care and life insurance combination products. Several well-known insurance companies offer products that, in exchange for a lump-sum premium deposit, will provide a long-term care benefit if it's needed and, if long-term care isn't needed, a life insurance death benefit instead. For example, a hypothetical $100,000 deposit at age 60 may pay $300,000 of lifetime benefits for long-term care expenses if needed, and if long-term care isn't needed, pay a life insurance death benefit of $150,000 to beneficiaries instead.[12]

The main benefit of this strategy is that even if long-term care isn't needed, life insurance death benefit will pay out to benefi-

---

[12] This is a hypothetical example and isn't representative of any specific product or policy.

ciaries, so the premium isn't entirely lost. Since there is medical underwriting involved, these products will not be an option in all cases, especially in situations where pre-existing medical conditions exist.

Accelerated death benefits. Some life insurance policies allow policyholders to receive an advance of their policy's death benefit while they're still alive. This early access to the death benefit is usually contingent on meeting certain requirements related to having very poor health. Requirements may include being confined to a nursing home, being terminally ill or not being able to perform several of the activities of daily living (ADLs). While some life insurance policies include this option at little or no additional cost, others do not. To determine if this option exists with an existing life insurance policy, review the policy contract or contact the insurance company.

Downsizing. In a situation where there's enough equity built up, either downsizing or selling the home can help pay for long-term care expenses. Downsizing or selling a home results in transferring an illiquid asset to cash. Using these funds to help pay for long-term care expenses may help preserve other assets such as IRA accounts, 401(k) accounts and investment accounts for a surviving spouse or for future generations.

Care from family. Depending on the level of care needed, receiving help from family members or friends can substantially reduce out-of-pocket long-term care expenses. While medical professionals are needed to provide certain long-term care related services, family members helping out with services that don't necessarily require a trained medical professional can help control costs.

Medicaid. Medicaid is a state-administered program that will pay for long-term care expenses once countable assets and income are below certain thresholds. Countable asset and income thresholds vary by state. Also, what's considered as a "countable" asset varies by state. You don't necessarily need to be financially destitute to qualify for Medicaid. Medicaid Trusts, or Asset Protection Trusts, can be used to bring assets and income below the threshold to qualify for Medicaid. By doing so, Medicaid pays the cost of long-term care. These types of trusts can be expensive and very rigid, and they require planning well in advance of needing long-term care, but they can make sense for a small percentage of people. A state-specific elder care attorney needs to be engaged to discuss these trusts in more detail.

REDUCING HEALTH CARE COSTS WITH HEALTHY LIVING

During this chapter, we've discussed important financial steps that can help control health care costs in retirement, such as using either a Medicare Advantage Plan or Medicare Supplement Plan to fill the gaps in Medicare Parts A and B, and carefully evaluating options to plan for long-term care expenses. These steps can help reduce the risk that out-of-control medical expenses will cause you to run out of money in retirement.

In addition to these items, another way to help control health care costs is to embrace healthy living. This probably isn't the first time you've heard that living an active lifestyle full of regular exercise and a good diet can lead to better health. Those who lead an active life during retirement not only tend to experience a greater level of overall satisfaction and happiness, but they also may spend less on health care costs each year. Because rising health care costs pose a formidable challenge to effective retirement planning today, anything you can do to keep those costs under control certainly helps with your overall planning.

SELF-ASSESSMENT: HEALTH CARE PLANNING

Health care planning's role is to help select appropriate coverage and take steps to control costs throughout retirement. The self-assessment below will ask you five questions to help you assess where you stand today with Health Care Planning. The confidence score displayed at the end of the assessment will provide you with instant feedback.

To access the self-assessment, enter the web address exactly as it appears here into your browser: **healthcare.rolekretirement.com**

(*Note:* Be sure the web address is entered in your browser *exactly* as it appears above without www., http://, or https://, or any other characters included in the web address line.)

Health Care Planning confidence score: _____

HOW CAN YOU APPLY FOR A PRIVATE CONSULTATION?

In the final chapter of the book, we'll discuss how to apply for a private consultation. During the consultation, you'll have a chance to request help with your own retirement planning. Read on to learn more.

FOLLOW-UP ITEMS

While reading the chapter and taking the self-assessment, did any items come to mind that you think you should follow up on? Use this section to make a note of these.

_____

_____

_____

_____

_____

_____

_____

_____

_____

_____

_____

_____

CHAPTER 7

ESTATE PLANNING

- Who will make decisions on your behalf if you become incapacitated?
- What are the downsides of the probate process?
- Which of your assets would go through the probate process as of today?
- How can you strengthen your estate plan?
- How can you leave a legacy that makes a positive impact on the lives of others?

Estate planning isn't just for the super rich. All people should go through estate planning. A lack of estate planning can place an unnecessary burden on survivors, result in conflicts within a family, and cause the wealth of knowledge and experiences accumulated throughout your life to dissolve at death. Avoiding these problems is addressed in Step 7 of comprehensive retirement planning, Estate Planning. Effective estate planning minimizes stress on survivors, transfers assets efficiently, and leaves a legacy that makes a positive impact on the lives of others. This chapter covers the essential components of estate planning.

INCAPACITY PLANNING

Incapacity planning addresses how decisions will be made on your behalf if you're unable to make them yourself. Without incapacity planning, family members may be left guessing about how you would have wanted important decisions handled. At the very least, this guessing game will place stress on loved ones. In worst-case scenarios, it can cause conflicts to arise in a family that can be hard to heal. Effective incapacity planning can take a tremendous amount of pressure off survivors at a very difficult time.

Following is a list of important documents related to incapacity planning. A state-specific elder care attorney can draft documents to meet your unique needs. Because laws related to incapacity planning vary from state to state, if you move states during retirement, it's important to review the documents with an elder care attorney familiar with the laws in the new state.

- **Durable Power of Attorney.** This document allows you to appoint a person to make financial decisions for you if you are unable to do so yourself. For example, someone who has been assigned durable power of attorney authorization can often handle decisions such as which accounts should be used first to pay medical bills.
- **Health Care Proxy.** This document appoints a person to make health care decisions for you if you are unable to do so yourself. For example, someone who has been assigned health care proxy authorization can often provide instructions to medical care providers on your behalf.
- **Living Will.** A living will documents your wishes about being kept alive in the case of terminal illness or persistent unconsciousness. This can protect family members from being put in the difficult position of having to guess what your wishes would have been.

- **Declaration of Anatomical Gift Form.** This form allows you to clarify your wishes regarding organ donation and becoming a subject of medical research.

WILLS AND PROBATE

One of the first estate planning steps many people take is to create a will. If you die without a will, some assets will be transferred at death according to state law. At the very least, this will result in a lengthy, expensive, and often frustrating state review process. In the worst case, people you want to receive assets may be disinherited entirely in favor of someone else who the state determines is a rightful heir.

However, while a will can be used to designate recipients of certain types of property, wills have their own set of challenges. Assets passed by will must first go through a state-court review process called probate. People who have inherited probated assets know firsthand how difficult the state-run probate process can be.

Here are some of the main downsides of the probate process:

- **It takes time.** The probate process can take years to complete. Since it's a court-run procedure, processing times vary widely depending on the court systems in your area. Assets that pass through probate can be stuck in the court review process for extended time periods.
- **It's public record.** Because matters that pass through court systems are public, your probated assets will become a searchable public record. People may be able to look up how much you had in probate, where it went, and other personal information that's better kept private.
- **It's expensive.** Courts may charge fees between 3% and 8% of the probated estate's value. This can place a substantial dent in a legacy.

AVOIDING PROBATE

As a result of the downsides of probate mentioned above, avoiding it when possible is often beneficial. Avoiding probate can result in assets passing where you want them to go much more efficiently, without any publicity, and often without any cost. Effective estate planning can help with avoiding probate.

A list of general strategies to avoid probate is included below. However, laws related to probate vary from state to state. Consult with a qualified attorney in your specific state to receive personalized advice on this important matter. Here are some methods commonly used to avoid probate:

Beneficiary designations

Assets that have beneficiaries assigned generally avoid probate. Often times, this category captures the bulk of the assets. Retirement accounts such as 401(k), 403(b), 457, and IRAs all have built-in features that allow beneficiary designations to be assigned. In addition, life insurance policies and annuities also allow for assigning beneficiaries. As long as beneficiaries are assigned, assets in these accounts will not go through the probate process.

When the account or policyholder passes away, the beneficiary generally needs to submit a death certificate to the investment custodian or insurance company to access the funds.

Because beneficiaries take precedence over a will, it's important to ensure that beneficiaries remain up to date. Updating a will while failing to update beneficiaries may result in unintended consequences. For example, Mary gets divorced and no longer wants assets to pass to her ex-spouse, so she updates her will and removes her ex-spouse. However, she fails to update the beneficiary designations on her 401k and IRA accounts, and her ex-spouse is left as the beneficiary. As a result, her ex-spouse may still receive her IRA and 401k accounts, even though she updated her will. If she had also updated her beneficiaries when updating her will, this challenge could have been avoided.

Payable-on-death (POD) and transfer-on-death (TOD) designations

For accounts that don't automatically allow for beneficiary assignments, payable-on-death (POD) or transfer-on-death (TOD) designations can be added. Adding a POD or TOD designation to an account works like adding a beneficiary and allows the account to pass to whomever you designate without needing to go through the probate process.

This applies most commonly to bank accounts and nonretirement accounts such as taxable investment accounts. Because most bank accounts, CDs, taxable investment accounts, and mutual fund accounts do not automatically request beneficiary designations to be set up when establishing the accounts, they may become probated unless a POD or TOD designation is added. The financial institution that your account is held with usually has a simple form that can be used to add a POD or TOD designation to any account at no cost. For help getting this form for your accounts, contact the institution where the account is held. At death, the person designated on the POD or TOD form can access the assets, usually by submitting a death certificate, without them needing to flow through the state-run probate process.

Joint tenants with right of survivorship (JTWROS)

Property or accounts owned as joint tenants with right of survivorship will transfer to the surviving joint owner without going through the probate process. However, adding a non-spouse joint owner to an account may trigger unintended tax consequences. If the goal is simply to avoid probate, adding a POD or TOD designation to the account may accomplish this with less complexity.

Revocable trusts

Transferring assets into a revocable trust will also avoid the probate process. This type of trust allows the person who creates it to maintain control over the asset during life and establish terms and conditions for how the assets will be distributed at death.

The previous options discussed that can be used to avoid probate will provide the beneficiary with a lump sum of money, no strings attached. In some cases, that may be fine. In others, if a higher level of control is desired, a revocable trust can be effective. For example, if someone wants assets to be distributed slowly over a period of years or to be used only for a specific purpose, such as education or health care, that be accomplished with a revocable trust. A qualified attorney can help with creating and customizing a revocable trust to meet you unique needs.

Irrevocable Trusts

Irrevocable trusts also avoid probate. With an irrevocable trust, a person transfers assets into a trust and surrenders control over the assets. Depending on how the trust is set up, they may be able to retain some use of the assets and income rights during life even after the assets are in the trust. Irrevocable trusts can be used as part of a strategy to address estate taxes and inheritance taxes. They can also be used to as part of a strategy to shield personal assets from long-term care expenses.

An asset-protection trust, also called a Medicaid trust, is a specific type of irrevocable trust that can be used to help someone qualify for Medicaid. When assets and income are below a certain threshold, the government-run Medicaid program pays for long-term care expenses. However, people who have assets above these thresholds can also qualify for Medicaid with effective pre-planning.

By depositing assets into a Medicaid trust, because control over the assets is surrendered to the trust, the assets contributed may no longer be considered as "countable" for Medicaid-eligibility purposes. As a result, countable assets and income may be reduced to a point that allows the person to qualify for Medicaid. If they do qualify, the Medicaid program will pay for long-term care expenses. The end result is that assets are protected from being depleted by long-term care and may be preserved for future generations.

Assets have to go in to the Medicaid trust at least five years prior to applying for Medicaid. These trusts are very rigid, usually expensive to set up and maintain, and have very strict, state-specific guidelines. Establishing and maintaining a Medicaid trust requires the help of an experienced elder care attorney who is familiar with Medicaid laws in your specific state.

REVIEWING YOUR ESTATE PLAN REGULARLY

Reviewing your estate plan every few years will help ensure that it remains aligned with your wishes. In addition to scheduled periodic reviews, the estate plan should be updated as soon as possible when certain life events occur. Here are some examples of life events that may warrant immediate updates to the estate plan:

- Marriage or divorce
- Birth of a child
- Children reaching age 18
- Death of a beneficiary
- Significant new assets acquired, such as real estate property or an inheritance
- Moving to a different state
- New legislation
- Changing your mind about a beneficiary or power-of-attorney designation

When engaging in comprehensive retirement planning, periodic reviews of the estate plan are built into the ongoing review process of the comprehensive plan as a whole.

LEAVING A LEGACY

The initial focus of comprehensive retirement planning is figuring out how to put yourself in the best position to live the life you want in retirement without having to worry about running out of money. Once that aspect of the plan is solidified, the focus often becomes how to leave a legacy that makes a positive impact in the lives of others. Leaving a legacy means different things to different people.

While part of leaving a legacy might be about transferring money, it's also important not to overlook the value in transferring knowledge and experiences. Especially after reaching retirement age, channeling the wealth of knowledge and experiences you've accumulated throughout life towards a greater good can make a significant impact on the lives of others.

How to pursue that depends on each person's unique set of experiences, interests, and passions. Here are a just few examples:

- Mentoring youth
- Spending time with underprivileged families
- Working with religious organizations
- Helping special needs children and adults
- Teaching your skills and talents to others
- Spending more time with younger generations of your family

This will help others, and it will also help you. Helping others contributes to an ongoing sense of purpose, fulfillment, and belonging throughout retirement. This ties the final step of comprehensive retirement planning, Estate Planning, back to where we started in step one, Lifestyle Planning. Good comprehensive retirement planning ties everything together.

SELF-ASSESSMENT: ESTATE PLANNING

Estate planning's role is to minimize stress on survivors, ensure that assets pass efficiently, and leave a legacy that makes a positive impact. The self-assessment below will ask you five questions to help you assess where you stand today with Estate Planning. The confidence score displayed at the end of the assessment will provide you with instant feedback.

To access the self-assessment, enter the web address exactly as it appears here into your browser: **estate.rolekretirement.com**

(*Note:* Be sure the web address is entered in your browser *exactly* as it appears above without www., http://, or https://, or any other characters included in the web address line.)

Estate Planning confidence score: _____

HOW CAN YOU APPLY FOR A PRIVATE CONSULTATION?

In the final chapter of the book, we'll discuss how to apply for a private consultation. During the consultation, you'll have a chance to request help with your own retirement planning. Read on to learn more.

FOLLOW-UP ITEMS

While reading the chapter and taking the self-assessment, did any items come to mind that you think you should follow up on? Use this section to make a note of these.

_____

_____

_____

_____

_____

_____

_____

_____

_____

_____

_____

_____

_____

CHAPTER 8

TYING IT ALL TOGETHER

People heading into retirement and those who have recently retired face many of the same common problems and challenges. *"I'm concerned that I'll run out of money." "I don't know if I'm on the right track." "I have investments, but I don't really have a plan for how I'll use them to generate income in retirement." "I don't know how to make the most of Social Security." "I don't know how I'll handle taxes and health care costs." "I don't have an organized, comprehensive plan that I can actually understand."* Comprehensive retirement planning can help address these common problems and challenges.

HOW CAN YOU APPLY FOR A PRIVATE CONSULTATION?

All of the topics covered in this book are addressed through my firm's proprietary retirement planning process. After reading this book, if you'd like help building a comprehensive plan for your retirement, the next step is to apply for a private consultation. During the consultation, you'll have a chance to request help with your own retirement planning. Here's how to apply:

- **Step 1:** Go to apply.rolekretirement.com
- **Step 2:** Complete the application.

- **Step 3:** Wait for a response by email. It usually takes at least 48 hours to review applications.

The private consultation can be held either by web meeting or in-person depending on location and scheduling. They last up to 60 minutes. For married couples, it's highly encouraged that you attend together. If your application is accepted, you'll be emailed a checklist of items to prepare.

SELF-ASSESSMENT: AFTER

The self-assessment below will ask you ten questions to help you assess where you stand now that you have concluded the book. The confidence score displayed at the end of the assessment will provide you with instant feedback. Compare this score with your score at the start of the book.

To access the self-assessment, enter the web address exactly as it appears here into your browser: **after.rolekretirement.com**

(**Note:** Be sure the web address is entered in your browser *exactly* as it appears above without www., http://, or https://, or any other characters included in the web address line.)

After confidence score: _____

Helpful Resources

I've included a list of resources below. Have a resource that you would like to see added to this list? Email kyle.rolek@rolekretirement.com to request an addition.

Lifestyle Planning Resources:

- "Why a Sense of Purpose Is So Crucial in Retirement", Marc Freedman, *Wall Street Journal,* Oct 31, 2013. https://blogs.wsj.com/experts/2013/10/31/why-a-sense-of-purpose-is-so-crucial-in-retirement/
- "5 Tips to Finding Meaning and Purpose in Later Life", Ed Merck, Next Avenue, Aug 13, 2014. http://www.nextavenue.org/5-tips-find-meaning-and-purpose-later-life/
- "Having a Sense of Purpose May Add Years To Your Life", Patrick Hill, The Association for Psychological Science, May 12, 2014. https://www.psychologicalscience.org/news/releases/having-a-sense-of-purpose-in-life-may-add-years-to-your-life.html
- "The Retirement Problem: What Will You Do With All That Time?", Stewart Friedman, Knowledge @ Wharton,

Jan 14, 2016.
http://knowledge.wharton.upenn.edu/article/the-
retirement-problem-what-will-you-do-with-all-that-time/

EXPENSE PLANNING RESOURCES:

- AARP Budget Worksheet
  http://www.aarp.org/content/dam/aarp/money/budgetin
  g_savings/2014-08/budgeting-worksheet-aarp.pdf
- US Bureau of Labor Statistics CPI Inflation Calculator
  https://www.msn.com/en-
  us/money/tools/timevalueofmoney
- AARP Health Care Cost Calculator
  https://www.aarp.org/retirement/the-aarp-health care-
  costs-calculator/

INCOME PLANNING RESOURCES:

- Social Security Retirement Planner, Social Security.
  Administration https://www.ssa.gov/planners/retire/
- Set up a Social Security account online, Social Security.
  Administration https://www.ssa.gov/myaccount/
- "Survivors Planner: Survivors Benefits for Your Widow or
  Widower", Social Security Administration.
  https://www.ssa.gov/planners/survivors/onyourown2.html

INVESTMENT PLANNING RESOURCES:

- "The Bucket Approach to Retirement Allocation",
  Christine Benz, Morningstar. Sep 19, 2016.
  http://www.morningstar.com/articles/714223/the-
  bucket-approach-to-retirement-allocation.html

TAX PLANNING RESOURCES:

- "Frequently Asked Questions: Retirement Income", AARP, Jan 2015. http://www.aarp.org/money/taxes/info-05-2010/faq_retirement_income.html
- "Pay Less Taxes in Retirement", Eileen Ambrose, AARP, Mar 2017. https://www.aarp.org/money/taxes/info-2017/pay-less-taxes-in-retirement.html
- "State-by-State Guide to Taxes on Retirees", Kiplinger, Nov 2017. https://www.kiplinger.com/tool/retirement/T055-S001-state-by-state-guide-to-taxes-on-retirees/index.php

HEALTH CARE PLANNING RESOURCES:

- "Medigap vs. Medicare Advantage", Consumer Reports, Oct. 14 2014. https://www.consumerreports.org/cro/news/2014/10/medigap-vs-medicare-advantage-consumer-reports/index.htm
- "I'm New to Medicare. Should I Sign Up For a Medigap/Medicare Supplement Plan?" National Council on Aging, May 17, 2016. https://www.mymedicarematters.org/2016/05/which-better-medigap-or-medicare-advantage/
- "Understanding Long-Term Care Insurance", AARP, May 2016. http://www.aarp.org/health/health-insurance/info-06-2012/understanding-long-term-care-insurance.html
- "Long-Term Care Calculator: Compare Costs, Types of Services in Your Area", AARP. http://www.aarp.org/relationships/caregiving-resource-center/LTCC/
- "The Troubling AARP Long-Term Care Scorecard", Richard Eisenberg, Next Avenue, June 14 2017.

http://www.nextavenue.org/aarp-long-term-care-scorecard/

- "Health Savings Account (HSA)", Health care.gov. https://www.health care.gov/glossary/health-savings-account-hsa/

LEGACY PLANNING RESOURCES:

- "Cost-Effective Wills", AARP, Lynnette Khalfani-Cox. http://www.aarp.org/money/estate-planning/info-03-2011/cost-effective-wills.html
- "Using Trusts to Qualify For Medicaid", Tara Lynne Groth, Next Avenue. Oct. 24, 2017. http://www.nextavenue.org/medicaid-trust-qualify-medicaid/
- "11 Quotes About Leaving a Legacy", SUCCESS, Lydia Sweatt, Dec. 08, 2016. http://www.success.com/article/11-quotes-about-leaving-a-legacy
- "Just the Basics: Asset Protection Trusts." http://www.paelderlaw.com/just-the-basics-asset-protection-trusts/

CONTACT US

All of the topics covered in this book are addressed through my firm's proprietary retirement planning process. After reading this book, if you'd like help building a comprehensive plan for your retirement, the next step is to apply for a private consultation. You can apply at **apply.rolekretirement.com**.

To discuss booking a private adult-education course for your company's employees or your organization's members, please get in touch using the contact information listed below:

Email: kyle.rolek@rolekretirement.com
Main office phone: (267) 427-5667
Website: www.rolekretirement.com
Mail: 30 S 15th Street, 15th floor,
Philadelphia, PA 19102

ABOUT THE AUTHORS

Kyle teaches adult education courses about retirement planning at prominent colleges and universities in the Greater Philadelphia area. He also works privately as an advisor to individual clients. His clients are those who want help organizing the various aspects of retirement into one simple, comprehensive plan.

Teaching courses was a natural outgrowth from growing up in a family of educators. His mom Kathy is a recently retired career-long elementary school special education teacher. His dad Ken and brother Kory are both active teachers and also coach track and field and cross-country.

Kyle graduated in 2009 from Lafayette College in Easton, Pennsylvania, with a degree in economics and business, where he was also a member of the track and field team. Before attending Lafayette College, he graduated from Wilson Area High School, located in the Lehigh Valley area of Pennsylvania, where he also ran track and played football.

He got his start as an advisor in 2009 with a Fortune 500 leader in the financial services industry. After consistently ranking as a top performer, he left that firm and started Rolek Retirement Planning, an independent Registered Investment Advisor, to be in a better position to provide unbiased advice to the firm's clients for the long term.

R odney A. Brooks has had a long and distinguished career in financial journalism. After receiving a B.S. degree from Cornell University, he became a top editor of USA Today's Money section, a position he held for nearly 30 years. He has written retirement or personal finance columns for the *Washington Post, USA TODAY, US News & World Report, ESPN's The Undefeated, Black Enterprise Magazine,* The Street.com, and MarketWatch. You will find his most recent articles at www.RodneyABrooks.com.

38697759R00074

Made in the USA
Columbia, SC
07 December 2018